CONTENTS

12

14

35

2

BABY JACKET SET

Easy

SIZES
Newborn (3 months, 6–12 months).

MEASUREMENTS
Chest 17 (20, 21)"/43 (51, 53.5)cm

MATERIALS
Yarn

Bernat® Baby Sport™, 12.3oz/350g skeins, each approx 1256yd/1148m (acrylic)
- 1 skein* in #21420 Baby Pink

** makes 4 (3, 3) sets*

Hook
- Size G/6 (4mm) crochet hook, *or size needed to obtain gauge*

Notions
- 1 button

GAUGE
16 dc and 8 rows = 4"/10cm using size G/6 (4mm) hook. *TAKE TIME TO CHECK GAUGE.*

CARDIGAN
Note Ch 3 at beg of row or rnd counts as dc.

Beg at neck edge, ch 46 (54, 54).

1st row (RS): 1 dc in 4th ch from hook. 1 dc in each of next 5 (6, 6) ch. (1 dc. Ch 1. 1 dc—V-st made) in next ch. 1 dc in each of next 6 (8, 8) ch. V-st in next ch. 1 dc in each of next 14 (16, 16) ch. V-st in next ch. 1 dc in each of next 6 (8, 8) ch. V-st in next ch. 1 dc in each of last 7 (8, 8) ch. Turn.

2nd to 6th (8th, 8th) rows: Ch 3. *1 dc in each dc to ch-1 sp of next V-st. V-st in ch-1 sp of next V-st. Rep from * 3 times more. 1 dc in each dc to end of row. Turn. 88 (112, 112) dc and 4 ch-1 sps at end of 6th (8th, 8th) row.

Divide Sleeves and Body
Next row (RS): Ch 3. 1 dc in each of next 12 (15, 15) dc. 1 dc in ch-1 sp of next V-st. Ch 6 (6, 8) for underarm. Skip next 18 (24, 24) dc for Sleeve. 1 dc in ch-1 sp of next V-st. 1 dc in each of next 26 (32, 32) dc. 1 dc in ch-1 sp of next V-st. Ch 6 (6, 8) for underarm. Skip next 18 (24, 24) dc for Sleeve. 1 dc in ch-1 sp of next V-st. 1 dc in each of last 13 (16, 16) dc. Turn.

Next row: Ch 3. 1 dc in each dc or ch to end of row. Turn. 68 (80, 84) dc.

Next row: Ch 3. 1 dc in each dc to end of row. Turn.

Rep last row until work from underarm ch measures 5 (5½, 6½)"/12.5 (14, 16.5)cm. Fasten off.

Sleeves
1st rnd (RS): Join yarn with sl st to center of underarm ch. Ch 3. 1 dc in each ch or dc around. 24 (30, 32) dc. Join.

2nd rnd: Ch 3. 1 dc in each dc around. Join.

Rep last rnd until work from underarm ch measures 4½ (5½, 6)"/ 11.5 (14, 15)cm. Fasten off.

Button Band
1st row (RS): Join yarn with sl st at corner of Left Front neck edge. Ch 1. Work 1 row of sc evenly down front edge. Turn.

2nd and 3rd rows: Ch 1. 1 sc in each sc to end of row. Turn. Fasten off.

Buttonhole Band
1st row (RS): Join yarn with sl st at lower corner of Right Front edge. Ch 1. Work 1 row of sc evenly up front edge. Turn.

2nd row: Ch 1. 1 sc in first sc. Ch 1. Skip next sc. 1 sc in each sc to end of row. Turn.

3rd row: Ch 1. 1 sc in each sc and ch-1 sp to end of row. Fasten off.

HAT
Note: Ch 2 at beg of rnd does not count as st.

Beg at crown, ch 3.

1st rnd: 8 hdc in 3rd ch from hook. Join with sl st to first hdc.

BABY JACKET SET

2nd rnd: Ch 2. 2 hdc in each hdc around. Join with sl st to first hdc. 16 hdc.

3rd rnd: Ch 2. *2 hdc in next hdc. 1 hdc in next hdc. Rep from * around. Join with sl st to first hdc. 24 hdc.

4th rnd: Ch 2. *1 hdc in each of next 2 hdc. 2 hdc in next hdc. Rep from * around. Join with sl st to first hdc. 32 hdc.

5th rnd: Ch 2. *2 hdc in next hdc. 1 hdc in each of next 3 hdc. Rep from * around. Join with sl st to first hdc. 40 hdc.

Size Newborn Only

6th rnd: Ch 2. *2 hdc in next hdc. 1 hdc in each of next 9 hdc. Rep from * around. Join with sl st to first hdc. 44 hdc.

Sizes 3 Months and 6–12 Months Only

6th rnd: Ch 2. *1 hdc in each of next 3 hdc. 2 hdc in next hdc. Rep from * around. Join with sl st to first. 50 hdc.

Size 6–12 Months Only

7th rnd: Ch 2. *2 hdc in next hdc. 1 hdc in each of next 7 hdc. Rep from * to last 2 hdc. 1 hdc in each of last 2 hdc. Join with sl st to first hdc. 56 hdc.

All Sizes

Next rnd: Ch 2. 1 hdc in each hdc around. Join with sl st to first hdc. 44 (50, 56) hdc.

Rep last rnd until Hat measures approx 4 (4½, 5)"/10 (11.5, 12.5)cm.

Next rnd: Ch 1. 1 sc in each hdc around. Join with sl st to first sc. Fasten off.

Ears (make 2)

Ch 5 (6, 6).

1st rnd: 1 sc in 2nd ch from hook. 1 sc in each of next 2 (3, 3) ch. 3 sc in last ch. Working into opposite side of ch, 1 sc in each of next 2 (3, 3) ch. 2 sc in last ch. Join with sl st to first sc. 10 (12, 12) sc.

2nd rnd: Ch 1. 1 sc in same sp as last sl st. 1 sc in each of next 3 (4, 4) sc. 3 sc in next sc. 1 sc in each of next 4 (5, 5) sc. 3 sc in last sc. Join with sl st to first sc. 14 (16, 16) sc.

3rd rnd: Ch 1. 1 sc in same sp as last sl st. 1 sc in each of next 4 (5, 5) sc. 3 sc in next sc. 1 sc in each of next 6 (7, 7) sc. 3 sc in next sc. 1 sc in last sc. Join with sl st to first sc. 18 (20, 20) sc.

4th to 6th rnds: Ch 1. 1 sc in same sp as last sl st. 1 sc in each sc around. Join with sl st to first sc. Fasten off leaving a long end to sew Ear to Hat.

Fold Ear flat. Sew Ears to Hat as shown in photo.•

LIKE A FOX BLANKET

Easy

MEASUREMENTS

Approx 50 x 30"/127 x 76cm, excluding hood

MATERIALS

Yarn

Bernat® Softee® Baby Chunky™, 5oz/140g skeins, each approx 155yd/142m (acrylic)

- 6 skeins in #96013 Creamsicle (MC)
- 1 skein each in #96006 Cream Puff (A) and #96017 Nighty Night (B)

Hooks

- Sizes H/8 (5mm) and L/11 (8mm) crochet hooks,

or size needed to obtain gauge

GAUGE

10 sts and 12 rows = 4"/10cm in pat using larger hook.
TAKE TIME TO CHECK GAUGE.

NOTE

To join new color, work to last loops on hook of first color. Yoh with new color, draw through loops and proceed with new color.

BLANKET

With larger hook and B, ch 126.

1st row (RS): 1 sc in 2nd ch from hook. *Ch 1. Skip next ch. 1 sc in next ch. Rep from * to end of ch. Turn. 125 sts.

2nd row: Ch 1. 1 sc in first sc. 1 sc in next ch-1 sp. *Ch 1. Skip next sc. 1 sc in next ch-1 sp. Rep from * to last sc. 1 sc in last sc. Break B. Join A. Turn.

3rd row: With A, ch 1. 1 sc in first sc. *Ch 1. Skip next sc. 1 sc in next ch-1 sp. Rep from * to last 2 sc. Ch 1. Skip next sc. 1 sc in last sc. Turn.

4th row: With A, as 2nd row.

Last 2 rows form pat.

With A, work 4 more rows in pat.

With MC, cont in pat until work from beg measures approx 30"/76cm, ending on a WS row. Fasten off.

Hood

1st row (RS): With larger hook, join MC with sl st to 49th st of last row of Blanket. Ch 1. 1 sc in same sp as last sl st. 1 sc in each of next 26 sts. Turn. 27 sts.

2nd row: Ch 1. 1 sc in each sc to end of row. Turn.

3rd row: Ch 1. 1 sc in each of next 8 sc. 2 sc in each of next 2 sc. 1 sc in each of next 7 sc. 2 sc in each of next 2 sc. 1 sc in each of next 8 sc. Turn. 31 sc.

4th to 8th rows: Ch 1. 1 sc in each sc to end of row. Turn.

9th row: Ch 1. (1 sc in each of next 9 sc. 2 sc in each of next 2 sc) twice. 1 sc in each of next 9 sc. Turn. 35 sc.

10th to 14th rows: Ch 1. 1 sc in each sc to end of row. Turn.

15th row: Ch 1. 1 sc in each of next 10 sc. 2 sc in each of next 2 sc. 1 sc in each of next 11 sc. 2 sc in each of next 2 sc. 1 sc in each of next 10 sc. Turn. 39 sc.

Cont even in sc until Hood measures 8"/20.5cm, ending on a WS row. Fasten off.

LIKE A FOX BLANKET

Top Hood

1st row (RS): With larger hook, join MC with sl st to 13th st of last row of Hood. Ch 1. 1 sc in same sp as last sl st. 1 sc in each of next 12 sc. Turn. 13 sc.

2nd and 3rd rows: Ch 1. 1 sc in each sc to end of row. Turn.

4th row: Ch 1. Sc2tog. 1 sc in each sc to last 2 sc. Sc2tog. 11 sc. Turn.

5th to 7th rows: Ch 1. 1 sc in each sc to end of row. Turn.

8th row: Ch 1. Sc2tog. 1 sc in each sc to last 2 sc. Sc2tog. 9 sc. Turn.

9th and 10th rows: Ch 1. 1 sc in each sc to end of row. Break MC at end of last row. Join A. Turn.

11th to 14th rows: With A, ch 1. 1 sc in each sc to end of row. Turn. Fasten off at end of 14th row. Sew sides of Top Hood to rem sts at either side of last row of Hood.

Border

With RS facing and larger hook, join B with sl st to any corner of Blanket.

1st rnd: Ch 1. Work sc evenly around entire edge of Blanket and front opening of Hood, having 3 sc in each corner. Join with sl st to first sc.

2nd rnd: Ch 1. Work 1 sc in each sc around, having 3 sc in each corner. Join with sl st to first sc. Fasten off.

Eyes (make 2)

With smaller hook and A, ch 2.

1st rnd: 6 sc in 2nd ch from hook. Join with sl st to first sc. Fasten off. With B, embroider French Knot (see page 10) in center of Eye.

Nose

With smaller hook and B, ch 2.

1st rnd: 6 sc in 2nd ch from hook. Join with sl st to first sc. Fasten off.

Ears

Inner ears (make 2)

With smaller hook and A, ch 2.

1st row (RS): 5 sc in 2nd ch from hook. Turn.

2nd row: Ch 1. 2 sc in each sc across. 10 sc. Turn.

3rd row: Ch 1. 1 sc in each of first 4 sc. (1 hdc. 1 dc) in next sc. (1 dc. 1 hdc) in next sc. 1 sc in each of next 4 sc. Fasten off.

Outer ears (make 2)

With MC and smaller hook, make as given for Inner Ear.

With WS of Inner Ear and Outer ear facing each other, and RS of Inner Ear facing, join B with sl st to first sc.

1st row: Ch 1. Working through both thicknesses, 1 sc in each of first 4 sc. 2 hdc in next st. (2 dc. 1 tr) in next st. (1 tr. 2 dc) in next st. 2 hdc in next st. 1 sc in each of next 4 sts. Fasten off.

FINISHING

Sew Eyes, Nose and Ears to Hood as seen in picture.•

SQUARE BEARS

Easy

MEASUREMENTS

Approx 6½"/16.5cm long, excluding legs

MATERIALS

Yarn (4)

Bernat® Baby Blanket Tiny™, 3½oz/100g skeins; each approx 316 yd/288m (polyester)

- 1 skein in #14001 Brown Bear (A)
- 1 skein in #14009 Clear Sky OR #14004 Hush Pink OR #14008 Seedling (B)

Hook

- Size E/4 (3.5mm) crochet hook, *or size needed to obtain gauge*

Notions

- Stuffing
- Black embroidery thread for eyes and nose

GAUGE

18 sc and 19 rows = 4"/10cm using size E/4 (3.5mm) hook.
TAKE TIME TO CHECK GAUGE.

STITCH GLOSSARY

Dcbp Yoh and draw up a loop around post of next stitch at back of work, inserting hook from right to left. (Yoh and draw through 2 loops on hook) twice.

Dcfp Yoh and draw up a loop around post of next stitch at front of work, inserting hook from right to left. (Yoh and draw through 2 loops on hook) twice.

SQUARE BEAR

Front/Back (make 2)

With B, ch 23.

1st row (RS): 1 sc in 2nd ch from hook. 1 sc in each ch to end of ch. Turn. 22 sc.

2nd row: Ch 1. 1 sc in each sc to end of row. Turn.

Rep last row until piece measures approx 3½"/9cm, ending on a WS row.

Next row (RS): Ch 2 (counts as hdc). *Dcfp around next sc. Dcbp around next sc. Rep from * to last sc. 1 hdc in last sc. Turn.

Next row: Ch 2 (counts as hdc). *Dcfp around next st. Dcbp around next st. Rep from * to last hdc. 1 hdc in top of ch 2. Break B. Join A.

Head

1st row: With A, ch 1. 1 sc in each st to end of row. Turn.

2nd to 4th rows: Ch 1. 1 sc in each sc to end of row. Turn.

Shape head

Next row: Ch 1. Sc2tog. 1 sc in each sc to last 2 sc. Sc2tog. Turn. 20 sts.

Rep last row, dec 2 sts every row to 10 sts. Fasten off.

Arms (make 2)

**With A, ch 2.

1st rnd: 8 sc in 2nd ch from hook. Join with sl st to first sc.

2nd rnd: Ch 1. 2 sc in each sc around. Join with sl st to first sc. 16 sc.

3rd to 5th rnds: Ch 1. 1 sc in each sc around. Join with sl st to first sc.**

6th rnd: Ch 1. *Sc2tog. 1 sc in each of next 2 sc. Rep from * around. Break A, join B with sl st to first st. 12 sts.

7th rnd: With B, ch 1. 1 sc in each st around. Join with sl st to first sc.

8th rnd: Ch 1. 1 sc in each sc around. Join with sl st to first sc. Rep last rnd 6 times more, stuffing very lightly (to maintain floppiness of limbs) as you work. Fasten off at end of last rnd

Legs (make 2)

Work from ** to ** as given for Arms.

6th rnd: Ch 1. *Sc2tog. 1 sc in each of next 2 sc. Rep from * around. Join with sl st to first st. 12 sts.

7th rnd: Ch 1. 1 sc in each st around. Join with sl st to first st. Rep last rnd 7 times more, stuffing very lightly as you work. Fasten off at end of last rnd.

Ears (make 2)

With A, ch 10. Join with sl st to first ch.

1st rnd: Ch 1. 1 sc in each ch around. Join with sl st to first sc.

2nd rnd: Ch 1. 1 sc in each of next 4 sc. 2 sc in next sc. 1 sc in each sc to last sc. 2 sc in last sc. Join with sl st to first sc. 12 sc.

3rd and 4th rnds: Ch 1. 1 sc in each sc around. Join with sl st to first sc.

5th rnd: Ch 1. (Sc2tog. 1 sc in next sc) 4 times. Join with sl st to first st. 8 sts.

6th rnd: Ch 1. (Sc2tog) 4 times. Join with sl st to first st. 4 sts. Fasten off, leaving long end. Thread end through rem sts and draw up tightly. Fasten securely.

FINISHING

With WS of Front and Back facing each other, sew edges tog, leaving opening for stuffing. Stuff Body. Sew rem edge closed. Attach Arms and Legs. Sew Ears to top of Head. With Black embroidery thread, embroider eyes using French knots and nose using satin st.•

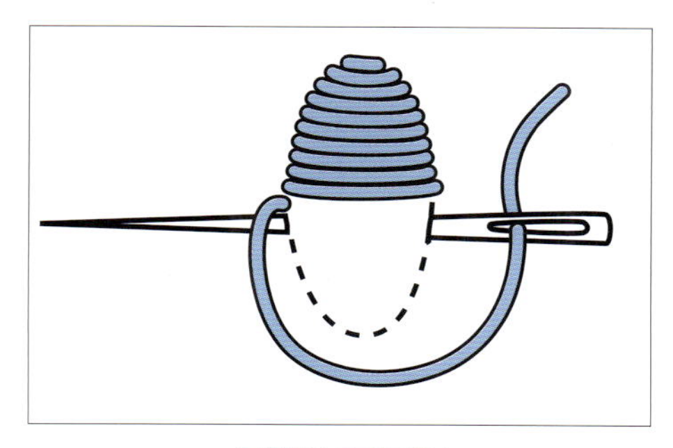

SATIN STITCH

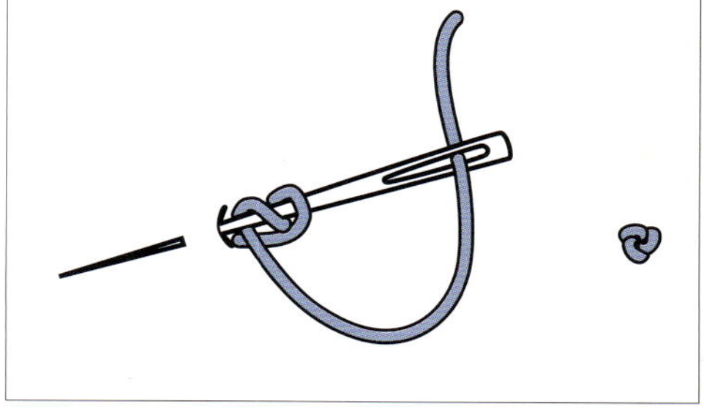

FRENCH KNOT

SLEEPY SLOTH LOVEY

Easy

MEASUREMENTS

Approx 22"/56cm square

MATERIALS

Yarn (4)

Bernat® Baby Blanket Tiny™, 3½oz/100g skeins, each approx 316 yd/288m (polyester)

• skein each in #14001 Brown Bear (A), #14002 Gray Owl (B), and #14003 Polar Bear (C)

Hook

• Size G/6 (4mm) crochet hook, *or size needed to obtain gauge*

Notions

• Stuffing

GAUGE

15 sc and 16 rows = 4"/10cm using size G/6 (4mm) hook. *TAKE TIME TO CHECK GAUGE.*

LOVEY

Body (Blanket)

With A, ch 83.

1st row (RS): 1 sc in 2nd ch from hook. *1 dc in next ch. 1 sc in next ch. Rep from * to last ch. 1 dc in last ch. Turn. 82 sts.

2nd row: Ch 1. 1 sc in first dc. *1 dc in next sc. 1 sc in next dc. Rep from * to last sc. 1 dc in last sc. Turn.

Rep 2nd row for pat until work from beg measures 22"/56cm, ending on a WS row. Fasten off.

Head

Note: Ch 2 at beg of rnds does not count as hdc.

With A, ch 3.

1st rnd: 10 hdc in 3rd ch from hook. Join with sl st to first hdc. 10 hdc.

2nd rnd: Ch 2. 2 hdc in each hdc around. Join with sl st to first hdc. 20 hdc.

3rd rnd: Ch 2. 1 hdc in first hdc. *2 hdc in next hdc. 1 hdc in next hdc. Rep from * to last hdc. 2 hdc in last hdc. Join with sl st to first hdc. 30 hdc.

4th rnd: Ch 2. 1 hdc in first hdc. 1 hdc in next hdc. *2 hdc in next hdc. 1 hdc in each of next 2 hdc. Rep from * to last hdc. 2 hdc in last hdc. Join with sl st to first hdc. 40 hdc.

5th to 10th rnds: Ch 2. 1 hdc in each hdc around. Join with sl st to first hdc.

11th rnd: Ch 2. *Hdc2tog. 1 hdc in each of next 2 hdc. Rep from * around. Join with sl st to first hdc. 30 hdc.

12th rnd: Ch 2. *Hdc2tog. 1 hdc in next hdc. Rep from * around. Join with sl st to first hdc. 20 hdc. Stuff Head.

13th rnd: Ch 2. (Hdc2tog) 10 times. Join with sl st to first st. 10 hdc. Fasten off.

Sew Head to center of Body.

FINISHING

Face

With C, ch 12.

1st rnd: 1 hdc in 3rd ch from hook. 1 hdc in each ch to last ch. 5 hdc in last ch. Working into opposite side of foundation ch, 1 hdc in each of next 8 ch. 4 hdc in last ch. Join with sl st to first hdc. 26 hdc.

2nd rnd: Ch 2. 1 hdc in each of first 10 hdc. 2 hdc in each of next 3 hdc. 1 hdc in each of next 10 hdc. 2 hdc in each of next 3 hdc. Join with sl st to first hdc. 32 hdc. Fasten off.

With A, embroider mouth and nose onto Face as shown in picture.

Eyes (make 2)

With B, ch 3.

1st rnd: 10 hdc in 3rd ch from hook. Join with sl st to first hdc. 10 hdc. Fasten off.

With C, embroider Eyes and sew Eyes onto Face as shown in picture. Sew completed Face to Head.

Feet (make 4)

With C, ch 3.

1st rnd: 8 hdc in 3rd ch from hook. Join with sl st to first hdc. 8 hdc.

2nd rnd: Ch 2. 2 hdc in each hdc around. Join with sl st to first hdc. 16 hdc.

3rd and 4th rnds: Ch 2. 1 hdc in each hdc around. Join with sl st to first hdc.

5th rnd: Ch 2. (Hdc2tog) 8 times. 8 hdc. Fasten off.

Sew one Foot to each corner of Body.•

BEAR CUB PONCHO

Easy

SIZES

6–12 (18–24) months.

MATERIALS

Yarn

Bernat® Pipsqueak™, 3½oz/100g skeins, each approx 101yd/91m (polyester)

- 2 skeins in #59012 Chocolate (MC)
- 1 skein in #59008 Vanilla (A)

Hook

- Size J/10 (6mm) crochet hook, *or size needed to obtain gauge*

GAUGE

9 sts and 9 rows = 4"/10cm in pat using size J/10 (6mm) hook.

TAKE TIME TO CHECK GAUGE.

PONCHO

With MC, ch 68 (72). Join with sl st to first ch to form ring, being careful not to twist chain.

1st rnd: Ch 1. 1 sc in first ch. Ch 1. Skip next ch. *1 sc in next ch. Ch 1. Skip next ch. Rep from * around. Join with sl st to first sc. 68 (72) sts.

2nd rnd: Sl st in first ch-1 sp. Ch 1. 1 sc in same sp as last sl st. Ch 1. Skip next sc. *1 sc in next ch-1 sp. Ch 1. Skip next sc. Rep from * around. Join with sl st to first sc.

Rep last rnd for pat until work from beg measures 3½ (5½)"/9 (14)cm.

Size 18–24 Months Only

Next rnd: Sl st in first ch-1 sp. Ch 1. Sc2tog over first and next ch-1 sps—2 sts decreased. (Ch 1. Skip next sc. 1 sc in next sc) 16 times. Ch 1. Skip next sc. Sc2tog over next 2 ch-1 sps. Ch 1. Skip next sc. (1 sc in next ch-1 sp. Ch 1. Skip next sc) to end of rnd. Join with sl st to first sc. 68 sts.

BEAR CUB PONCHO

Both Sizes

Shape yoke

1st rnd: Sl st in first ch-1 sp. Ch 1. Sc2tog over first and next ch-1 sps. (Ch 1. Skip next sc. 1 sc in next ch-1 sp) 7 times. Ch 1. Sc2tog over next 2 ch-1 sps. (Ch 1. Skip next sc. 1 sc in next ch-1 sp) 6 times. Ch 1. Sc2tog over next 2 ch-1 sps. (Ch 1. Skip next sc. 1 sc in next ch-1 sp) 7 times. Ch 1. Sc2tog over next 2 ch-1 sps. (Ch 1. Skip next sc. 1 sc in next ch-1 sp) 6 times. Ch 1. Skip last sc. Join with sl st to first sc. 60 sts.

2nd and alt rnds: Sl st in first ch-1 sp. Ch 1. 1 sc in same sp as last sl st. Ch 1. Skip next sc. *1 sc in next ch-1 sp. Ch 1. Skip next sc. Join with sl st to first sc.

3rd rnd: Sl st in first ch-1 sp. Ch 1. Sc2tog over first and next ch-1 sps. (Ch 1. Skip next sc. 1 sc in next ch-1 sp) 6 times. Ch 1. Sc2tog over next 2 ch-1 sps. (Ch 1. Skip next sc. 1 sc in next ch-1 sp) 5 times. Ch 1. Sc2tog over next 2 ch-1 sps. (Ch 1. Skip next sc. 1 sc in next ch-1 sp) 6 times. Ch 1. Sc2tog over next 2 ch-1 sps. (Ch 1. Skip next sc. 1 sc in next ch-1 sp) 5 times. Ch 1. Skip last sc. Join with sl st to first sc. 52 sts.

5th rnd: Sl st in first ch-1 sp. Ch 1. Sc2tog over first and next ch-1 sps. (Ch 1. Skip next sc. 1 sc in next ch-1 sp) 5 times. Ch 1. Sc2tog over next 2 ch-1 sps. (Ch 1. Skip next sc. 1 sc in next ch-1 sp) 4 times. Ch 1. Sc2tog over next 2 ch-1 sps. (Ch 1. Skip next sc. 1 sc in next ch-1 sp) 5 times. Ch 1. Sc2tog over next 2 ch-1 sps. (Ch 1. Skip next sc. 1 sc in next ch-1 sp) 4 times. Ch 1. Skip last sc. Join with sl st to first sc. 44 sts.

7th rnd: Sl st in first ch-1 sp. Ch 1. Sc2tog over first and next ch-1 sps. (Ch 1. Skip next sc. 1 sc in next ch-1 sp) 4 times. Ch 1. Sc2tog over next 2 ch-1 sps. (Ch 1. Skip next sc. 1 sc in next ch-1 sp) 3 times. Ch 1. Sc2tog over next 2 ch-1 sps. (Ch 1. Skip next sc. 1 sc in next ch-1 sp) 4 times. Ch 1. Sc2tog over next 2 ch-1 sps. (Ch 1. Skip next sc. 1 sc in next ch-1 sp) 3 times. Ch 1. Skip last sc. Join with sl st to first sc. 36 sts.

9th rnd: Sl st in first ch-1 sp. Ch 1. Sc2tog over first and next ch-1 sps. (Ch 1. Skip next sc. 1 sc in next ch-1 sp) 3 times. Ch 1. Sc2tog over next 2 ch-1 sps. (Ch 1. Skip next sc. 1 sc in next ch-1 sp) 2 times.

Ch 1. Sc2tog over next 2 ch-1 sps. (Ch 1. Skip next sc. 1 sc in next ch-1 sp) 3 times. Ch 1. Sc2tog over next 2 ch-1 sps. (Ch 1. Skip next sc. 1 sc in next ch-1 sp) 2 times. Ch 1. Skip last sc. Join with sl st to first sc. 28 sts.

10th rnd: Sl st in first ch-1 sp. Ch 1. 1 sc in same sp as last sl st. *Ch 1. Skip next sc. 1 sc in next ch-1 sp. Rep from * around. Do *not* join. Turn. 27 sts (14 sc and 13 ch-1 sps).

Shape Hood

Begin working in rows as follows:

Next row (WS): Ch 1. 1 sc in first sc. 1 sc in first ch-1 sp. (Ch 1. Skip next sc. 1 sc in next ch-1 sp) 4 times. Ch 1. Skip next sc. [(1 sc. Ch 1. 1 sc) in next ch-1 sp. Ch 1. Skip next sc.] 4 times. (1 sc in next ch-1 sp. Ch 1. Skip next sc) 3 times. 1 sc in next ch-1 sp. 1 sc in last sc. Turn. 35 sts.

Next row (RS): Ch 1. 1 sc in first st. Ch 1. Skip next sc. *1 sc in next ch-1 sp. Ch 1. Skip next sc. Rep from * to last sc. 1 sc in last sc. Turn.

Next row (WS): Ch 1. 1 sc in first sc. *1 sc in next ch-1 sp. Ch 1. Skip next sc. Rep from * to last ch-1 sp. 1 sc in last ch-1 sp. 1 sc in last sc. Turn.

Rep last 2 rows until Hood measures 8 (9)"/20.5 (23)cm, ending on a WS row.

Next row (RS): Ch 1. 1 sc in first st. Ch 1. Skip next sc. (1 sc in next ch-1 sp. Ch 1. Skip next sc) 6 times. (Sc2tog over next 2 ch-1 sps. Ch 1) twice. Ch 1. Skip next sc. (1 sc in next ch-1 sp. Ch 1. Skip next sc) 6 times. 1 sc in last sc. Turn. 31 sts.

Next row: Ch 1. 1 sc in first sc. *1 sc in next ch-1 sp. Ch 1. Skip next sc. Rep from * to last 2 sts. 1 sc in last ch-1 sp. 1 sc in last sc. Turn.

Next row: Ch 1. 1 sc in first st. Ch 1. Skip next sc. (1 sc in next ch-1 sp. Ch 1. Skip next sc) 5 times. (Sc2tog over next 2 ch-1 sps. Ch 1) twice. Skip next sc. (1 sc in next ch-1 sp. Ch 1. Skip next sc) 5 times. 1 sc in last sc. 27 sts. Fasten off.

Sew top Hood seam.

FINISHING

Ears (make 2 with MC and 2 with A)

Ch 2.

1st row: 6 sc in 2nd ch from hook. Turn.

2nd row: Ch 1. 2 sc in each sc to end of row. 12 sc. Fasten off.

Place one A Ear and one MC Ear tog with WS facing each other. With A Ear facing, join MC with sl st to first sc. Ch 1. Working through both thicknesses, work 1 sc in each sc to end of row. Fasten off. Rep for second Ear.

Sew Ears to top of Hood as seen in picture.•

CHARACTER SWEATERS

Easy

SIZES
6 (12, 18, 24) months.

MEASUREMENTS
Chest 19½ (21½, 23½, 25½)"/49.5 (54.5, 59.5, 65)cm

MATERIALS
Yarn
Bernat® Softee® Baby™, 5oz/140g skeins, each approx 362yd/331m (acrylic)
Kitty Version
• 1 (2, 2, 3) skeins in #30310 Mauve (A)
• 1 skein in #02001 Pink (B)
Bear Version
• 1 (2, 2, 3) skeins in #30111 Blue Jeans (A)
• 1 skein in #02004 Mint (B)

Hooks
• Size E/4 (3.5mm) and G/6 (4mm) crochet hooks, *or size needed to obtain gauge*

Notions
• 2 buttons for eyes.
• For Kitty Version only: Small amount of dark pink worsted-weight yarn for nose and mouth embroidery

GAUGE
16 sc and 19 rows = 4"/10cm using larger hook.
TAKE TIME TO CHECK GAUGE.

STITCH GLOSSARY
Dcbp Yoh and draw up a loop around post of next stitch at back of work, inserting hook from right to left. (Yoh and draw through 2 loops on hook) twice.
Dcfp Yoh and draw up a loop around post of next stitch at front of work, inserting hook from right to left. (Yoh and draw through 2 loops on hook) twice.

NOTES
1) Sweater is worked in one piece from neck edge down.
2) Ch 3 at beg of rnd counts as dc.
3) Ch 2 at beg of rnd counts as hdc.
4) To change colors, work to last loops on hook of stitch. Draw new color through last loops and proceed with new color.

SWEATER
Body
With larger hook and A, beg at neck edge, ch 56 (60, 64, 68) loosely (foundation ch needs to pull over baby's head). Join with sl st to first ch, taking care not to twist ch.
1st rnd: Ch 3. 1 dc in each of next 7 (8, 9, 10) ch. (1 dc. Ch 1. 1 dc—V-st made) in next ch. 1 dc in each of next 10 ch. V-st in next ch. 1 dc in each of next 16 (18, 20, 22) ch. V-st in next ch. 1 dc in each of next 10 ch. V-st in next ch. 1 dc in each of last 8 (9, 10, 11) ch. Join with sl st to top of ch 3.
2nd to 9th (10th, 11th, 12th) rnds: Ch 3. *1 dc in each dc to ch-1 sp of next V-st. V-st in ch-1 sp of next V-st. Rep from * 3 times more. 1 dc in each dc to end of rnd. Join. 124 (136, 148, 160) dc and 4 ch-1 sps at end of 9th (10th, 11th ,12th) rnd.

Divide sleeves and body
1st rnd: Ch 3. 1 dc in each of next 16 (18, 20, 22) dc. 1 dc in ch-1 sp of next V-st. Ch 3 for underarm. Skip next 28 (30, 32, 34) dc. 1 dc in ch-1 sp of next V-st. 1 dc in each of next 34 (38, 42, 46) dc. 1 dc in ch-1 sp of next V-st. Ch 3 for underarm. Skip next 28 (30, 32, 34) dc. 1 dc in ch-1 sp of next V-st. 1 dc in each of last 17 (19, 21, 23) dc. Join with sl st to top of ch 3.
2nd rnd: Ch 3. 1 dc in each dc or ch around. Break A, join B with sl st to top of ch 3. 78 (86, 94, 102) dc.
3rd rnd: With B, ch 2 (counts as hdc here and throughout). 1 hdc in each dc around. Join with sl st to top of ch 2.
4th rnd: Ch 2. 1 hdc in each hdc around. Join with sl st to top of ch 2.
Rep last rnd until section worked in B measures 2½ (3, 3, 4)"/6 (7.5, 7.5, 10)cm. Break B, join A.
Next rnd: With A, ch 3. 1 dc in each hdc around. Join with sl st to top of ch 3.

Next rnd: Ch 3. 1 dc in each dc around. Join with sl st to top of ch 3.
Rep last rnd until work from underarm measures 4½ (5½, 5½, 6)"/ 11.5 (14, 14, 15)cm.

Ribbing

1st rnd: Ch 2. *Dcbp around post of next st. Dcfp around post of next st. Rep from * to last st. Dcbp around post of last st. Join with sl st to top of ch 2.
Rep last rnd 4 (5, 5, 6) times more. Fasten off at end of last rnd.

Sleeves

1st rnd (RS): With larger hook, join A with sl st to center of underarm ch. Ch 3. 1 dc in each ch or dc around. Join with sl st to top of ch 3. 31 (35, 39, 43) dc.

2nd rnd: Ch 3. 1 dc in each dc around. Break A, join B with sl st to top of ch 3.

3rd rnd: With B, ch 2. 1 hdc in each dc around. Join with sl st to top of ch 2.

4th rnd: Ch 2. 1 hdc in each hdc around. Join with sl st to top of ch 2.
Rep last rnd until section worked in B measures 2½ (3, 3, 4)"/6 (7.5, 7.5, 10)cm. Break B, join A with sl st to top of ch 2.

Next rnd: With A, ch 3. 1 dc in each hdc around. Join with sl st to top of ch 3.

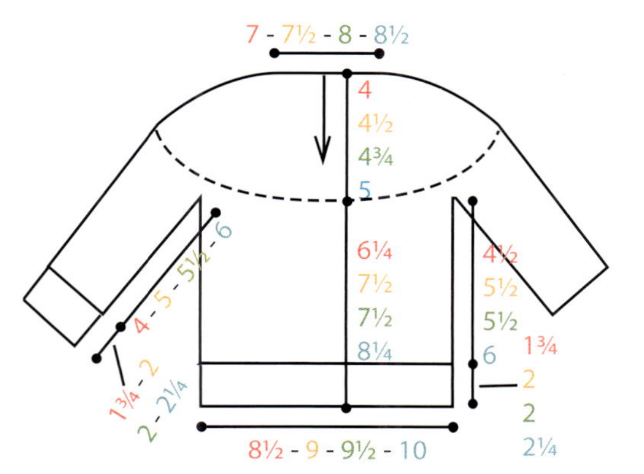

Next rnd: Ch 3. 1 dc in each dc around. Join with sl st to top of ch 3.
Rep last rnd until work from under-arm chain measures 4 (5, 5½, 6)"/10 (12.5, 14, 15)cm.

Next rnd: Ch 3. 1 dc in each of next 15 dc. Dc2tog. 1 dc in each dc to end of rnd. Break A, join B with sl st to top of ch 3. 30 (34, 38, 42) dc.

Ribbing

1st rnd: With B, ch 2 (counts as first st). *Dcbp around post of next st. Dcfp around post of next st. Rep from * to last st. Dcbp around post of last st. Join with sl st to top of ch 2.
Rep last rnd 4 (5, 5, 6) times more. Fasten off at end of last rnd.

Neck edging

1st rnd: Join B with sl st in center back rem ch of foundation ch. Ch 1. Work 1 sc in each rem ch around. Join with sl st to first sc.

2nd rnd: Ch 1. 1 sc in each sc around. Join with sl st to first sc. Fasten off.

FINISHING

Kitty Version

Ears (make 2)

With smaller hook and B, ch 8.

1st row: 1 sc in 2nd ch from hook. 1 sc in each ch to end of ch. Turn. 7 sc.

2nd row: Ch 1. 1 sc in each sc to end of row. Turn.

3rd row: Ch 1. Sc2tog. 1 sc in each of next 3 sc. Sc2tog. Turn. 5 sts.

4th row: Ch 1. Sc2tog. 1 sc in next sc. Sc2tog. Turn. 3 sts.

5th row: Ch 1. Sc3tog. Do *not* turn. Ch 1. Work 1 rnd of sc evenly around edges of Ear, having 3 sc in each corner. Join with sl st to first sc. Fasten off.

Bear Version

Ears (make 2)

With smaller hook and B, ch 4.

1st row: 7 dc in 4th ch from hook (ch 3 counts as dc). 8 dc.

2nd row: Ch 2 (counts as hdc). 1 hdc in first dc. 2 hdc in each dc to end of row. Fasten off. 16 hdc.

Both Versions

Attach Ears along top edge of contrast band of B on Front of sweater, making sure they are evenly spaced on each side edge. Sew buttons for eyes as shown in picture. Using A for Bear Version or dark pink worsted-weight yarn for Kitty Version, embroider nose and mouth as shown in picture•

CUDDLE BUNNIES

Easy

MEASUREMENTS

Approx 9"/23cm tall

MATERIALS

Yarn (5)

Bernat® Pipsqueak™, 3½oz/100g skeins, each approx 101yd/92m (polyester)

- 2 skeins in #59005 Whitey White (A)
- 2 skeins in #59745 Blue Ice* OR color of your choice (B)

*see Cuddle Bunny on left in photo

Hook

- Size I/9 (5.5mm) crochet hook,

or size needed to obtain gauge

Notions

- Stitch marker
- Stuffing

GAUGE

12 sc and 11 rows = 4"/10cm using size I/9 (5.5mm) hook.
TAKE TIME TO CHECK GAUGE.

NOTES

1) Ch 3 at beg of rnd counts as dc.

2) To join new color, work to last 2 loops on hook. Draw new color through last 2 loops then proceed in new color.

CUDDLE BUNNY

Head and Body

With A, ch 2.

1st rnd: 6 sc in 2nd ch from hook. Join with sl st to first sc.

2nd rnd: Ch 1. 2 sc in each sc around. Join with sl st to first sc. 12 sc.

3rd rnd: Ch 1. 1 sc in first sc. *2 sc in next sc. 1 sc in next sc. Rep from * to last sc. 2 sc in last sc. Join with sl st to first sc. 18 sc.

4th and alt rnds: Ch 1. 1 sc in each sc around. Join with sl st to first sc.

5th rnd: Ch 1. *1 sc in each of next 2 sc. 2 sc in next sc. Rep from * around. Join with sl st to first sc. 24 sc.

7th rnd: Ch 1. *1 sc in each of next 3 sc. 2 sc in next sc. Rep from * around. Join with sl st to first sc. 30 sc.

9th rnd: Ch 1. *1 sc in each of next 4 sc. 2 sc in next sc. Rep from * around. Join with sl st to first sc. 36 sc.

11th rnd: Ch 1. *1 sc in each of next 5 sc. 2 sc in next sc. Rep from * around. Join with sl st to first sc. 42 sc.

13th rnd: Ch 1. *1 sc in each of next 6 sc. 2 sc in next sc. Rep from * around. Join with sl st to first sc. 48 sc.

15th rnd: Ch 1. *1 sc in each of next 7 sc. 2 sc in next sc. Rep from * around. Join with sl st to first sc. 54 sc. Place marker at end of rnd.

16th rnd: Ch 1. 1 sc in each sc around. Join with sl st to first sc.

Rep last rnd until work from marked rnd measures 2"/5cm. Break A. Join B.

With B, rep last rnd for 3"/7.5cm more.

Stuff Head and Body lightly.

CUDDLE BUNNIES

Shape Bottom

1st rnd: With B, ch 1. *1 sc in each of next 7 sc. Sc2tog. Rep from * around. Join with sl st to first sc. 48 sts.

2nd rnd: Ch 1. *1 sc in each of next 6 sc. Sc2tog. Rep from * around. Join with sl st to first sc. 42 sts.

3rd rnd: Ch 1. *1 sc in each of next 5 sc. Sc2tog. Rep from * around. Join with sl st to first sc. 36 sts.

4th rnd: Ch 1. *1 sc in each of next 4 sc. Sc2tog. Rep from * around. Join with sl st to first sc. 30 sts.

5th rnd: Ch 1. *1 sc in each of next 3 sc. Sc2tog. Rep from * around. Join with sl st to first sc. 24 sts.

6th rnd: Ch 1. *1 sc in each of next 2 sc. Sc2tog. Rep from * around. Join with sl st to first sc. 18 sts. Stuff rem of Body.

7th rnd: Ch 1. *1 sc in next sc. Sc2tog. Rep from * around. Join with sl st to first sc. 12 sts. Fasten off, leaving a long end. Thread yarn through rem sts. Pull tightly and fasten securely.

Ears (make 2 each with A and B)

Ch 14.

1st row (RS): 1 sc in 2nd ch from hook. *Ch 1. Skip next ch. 1 sc in next ch. Rep from * to end of chain. Turn.

2nd row: Ch1. 1 sc in first sc.*1 sc in next ch-1 sp. Ch 1. Skip next sc. Rep from * to last last 2 sts. 1 sc in next ch-1 sp. 1 sc in last sc. Turn.

3rd row: Ch 1. 1 sc in first sc. *Ch 1. Skip next sc. 1 sc in next ch-1 sp. Rep from * to last 2 sc. Ch 1. Skip next sc. 1 sc in last sc. Turn.

Rep last 2 rows until work from beg measures approx 6"/15cm, ending on a 3rd row.

Shape top

1st row (WS): Ch 1. Skip first sc. *1 sc in next ch-1 sp. Ch 1. Skip next sc. Rep from * to last sc. Turn. Leave last sc unworked.

Rep last row until row: "**Next row:** Ch 1. Skip first sc. 1 sc in next ch 1-sp. Turn. Leave last sc unworked." has been worked.

Fasten off.

With WS tog, sew Ear A and Ear B tog.

Cheeks (make 2)

With A, ch 2.

1st rnd: 6 sc in 2nd ch from hook. Join with sl st to first sc.

2nd rnd: Ch 1. 2 sc in each sc around. Join with sl st to first sc. 12 sc.

3rd rnd: Ch 1.*1 sc in next sc. 2 sc in next sc. Rep from * around. Join with sl st to first sc. 18 sc. Fasten off.

Tail

With A, ch 2.

1st rnd: 7 sc in 2nd ch from hook. Join with sl st to first sc.

2nd rnd: Ch 1. 2 sc in each sc around. Join with sl st to first sc. 14 sc.

3rd rnd: Ch 1. *1 sc in next sc. 2 sc in next sc. Rep from * around. Join with sl st to first sc. 21 sc.

4th rnd: Ch 1. 1 sc in each sc around. Join with sl st to first sc.

5th rnd: Ch 1. *1 sc in next sc. Sc2tog. Rep from * around. Join with sl st to first sc. 14 sts. Fasten off.

FINISHING

Sew Ears to top of Head. Sew Cheeks in position, stuffing lightly. With B, embroider Nose and Eyes, using satin stitch. Stuff Tail lightly and sew to back of Body.•

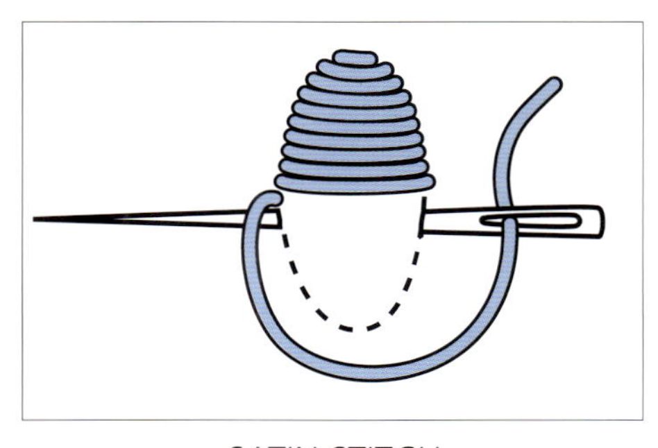

SATIN STITCH

KITTY BONNET

Easy

SIZES

6 (12, 18–24) months.

MATERIALS

Yarn

Bernat® Softee® Baby™, 5oz/140g skeins, each approx 362yd/331m (acrylic)

- 1 skein each in #30008 Antique White (A) and #30424 Soft Red (B)

Hook

- Size G/6 (4mm) crochet hook, *or size needed to obtain gauge*

GAUGE

16 sc and 19 rows = 4"/10cm using size G/6 (4mm) hook.
TAKE TIME TO CHECK GAUGE.

BONNET

With A, ch 3.

1st rnd: 12 hdc in 3rd ch from hook. Join with sl st to first hdc.

2nd rnd: Ch 2. 2 hdc in each hdc around. Join with sl st to first hdc. 24 hdc.

3rd rnd: Ch 2. 1 hdc in first hdc. *2 hdc in next hdc. 1 hdc in next hdc. Rep from * to last hdc. 2 hdc in last hdc. Join with sl st to first hdc. 36 hdc.

4th rnd: Ch 2. 2 hdc in first hdc. *1 hdc in each of next 2 hdc. 2 hdc in next hdc. Rep from * to last hdc. 1 hdc in last hdc. Join with sl st to first hdc. 48 hdc.

5th rnd: Ch 2. 2 hdc in first hdc. *1 hdc in each of next 11 (3, 2) hdc. 2 hdc in next hdc. Rep from * to last 11 (3, 2) hdc. 2 hdc in next hdc. 1 hdc in each of last 11 (3, 1) hdc. Join with sl st to first hdc. 52 (60, 64) hdc.

6th rnd: Ch 2. 1 hdc in each hdc around. Join with sl st to first hdc.

Rep last rnd until work from beg measures 4 (5, 5)"/10 (12.5, 12.5)cm.

First Earflap

Proceed in rows as follows:

****1st row:** Ch 2. 1 hdc in each of next 13 (15, 15) hdc. Turn. Leave rem hdc unworked.

2nd and 3rd rows: Ch 2. 1 hdc in each hdc to end of row. Turn.

4th row: Ch 2. Hdc2tog. 1 hdc in each of next 9 (11, 11) hdc. Hdc2tog. Turn.

5th row: Ch 2. Hdc2tog. 1 hdc in each of next 7 (9, 9) hdc. Hdc2tog. Turn.

6th row: Ch 2. Hdc2tog. 1 hdc in each of next 5 (7, 7) hdc. Hdc2tog. Turn.

Size 6 months only

Fasten off.**

Sizes 12 and 18–24 months only

7th row: Ch 2. Hdc2tog. 1 hdc in each of next 5 hdc. Hdc2tog. Fasten off.**

All sizes

Skip next 8 hdc. Join A with sl st to next hdc. Work from ** to ** as given for First Earflap.

Edging

Join B with sl st to center back hdc. Ch 1. Work 1 rnd of sc evenly around edge of Hat, working 3 sc in each corner. Join with sl st to first sc. Fasten off.

Outer Ear (make 2)

With A, ch 11.

1st row: 1 sc in 2nd ch from hook. 1 sc in each ch to end of ch. Turn. 10 sc.

2nd and 3rd rows: Ch 1. 1 sc in each sc across. Turn.

4th row: Ch 1. Sc2tog. 1 sc in each of next 6 sc. Sc2tog. Turn. 8 sts.

5th row: Ch 1. 1 sc in each st across. Turn.

6th row: Ch 1. Sc2tog. 1 sc in each of next 4 sc. Sc2tog. Turn. 6 sts.

7th row: Ch 1. 1 sc in each st across. Turn.

8th row: Ch 1. Sc2tog. 1 sc in each of next 2 sc.

Sc2tog. Turn. 4 sts.
9th row: Ch 1. (Sc2tog) twice. Turn.
10th row: Ch 1. Sc2tog. Fasten off.

Inner Ear (make 2)
With B, ch 9.
1st row: 1 sc in 2nd ch from hook. 1 sc in each ch to end of ch. Turn. 8 sc.
2nd and 3rd rows: Ch 1. 1 sc in each sc across. Turn.
4th row: Ch 1. Sc2tog. 1 sc in each of next 4 sc. Sc2tog. Turn. 6 sts.
5th row: Ch 1. Sc2tog. 1 sc in each of next 2 sc. Sc2tog. Turn. 4 sts.
6th row: Ch 1. (Sc2tog) twice. Turn.
7th row: Ch 1. Sc2tog. Fasten off

FINISHING

Sew Inner Ear to Outer Ear. Attach Ears to sides of Hat as shown in picture.•

BABY'S BUDDIES

Intermediate

BABY'S BUNNY BUDDY

MATERIALS

Yarn (4)

Lily® Sugar'n Cream, 2½oz/71g skeins, each approx 120yd/109m (cotton)

- 2 skeins in #00001 White (MC)
- 1 skein each in #01628 Hot Orange (B), #00084 Sage Green (C), and #00046 Rose Pink (D)
- Small amounts in #01130 Warm Brown (E) and #00082 Jute (F), for embroidery

Lily® Sugar'n Cream, 4oz/113g skeins, each approx 190yd/174m (cotton)

- 1 skein in #18083 Cornflower Blue (A)

Hook

- Size E/4 (3.5mm) crochet hook, *or size needed to obtain gauge*

Notions

- Stuffing

GAUGE

16 sc and 20 rows = 4"/10cm using size E/4 (3.5mm) hook.
TAKE TIME TO CHECK GAUGE.

Body

With MC, ch 2.

****1st rnd:** 7 sc in 2nd ch from hook. Join with sl st in first sc.

2nd rnd: Ch 1. 2 sc in each sc around. Join with sl st in first sc. 14 sc.

3rd rnd: Ch 1. 1 sc in same sp as last sl st. *2 sc in next sc. 1 sc in next sc. Rep from * to last sc. 2 sc in next sc. Join with sl st in first sc. 21 sc.

4th rnd: Ch 1. 1 sc in same sp as last sl st. *2 sc in next sc. 1 sc in each of next 2 sc. Rep from * to last 2 sc. 2 sc in next sc. 1 sc in next sc. Join with sl st in first sc. 28 sc.

5th rnd: Ch 1. 1 sc in same sp as last sl st. *2 sc in next sc. 1 sc in each of next 3 sc. Rep from * to last 3 sc. 2 sc in next sc. 1 sc in each of next 2 sc. Join with sl st in first sc. 35 sc.

6th rnd: Ch 1. 1 sc in same sp as last sl st. *2 sc in next sc. 1 sc in each of next 4 sc. Rep from * to last 4 sc. 2 sc in next sc. 1 sc in each of next 3 sc. Join with sl st in first sc. 42 sc.

7th rnd: Ch 1. 1 sc in same sp as last sl st. *2 sc in next sc. 1 sc in each of next 5 sc. Rep from * to last 5 sc. 2 sc in next sc. 1 sc in each of next 4 sc. Join with sl st in first sc. 49 sc.**

8th to 11th rnds: Ch 1. 1 sc in same sp as last sl st and each sc around. Join with sl st in first sc.

12th rnd: Ch 1. 1 sc in same sp as last sl st. *Draw up a loop in each of next 2 sc. Yoh and draw through 3 loops on hook—Sc2tog made. 1 sc in each of next 5 sc. Rep from * to last 6 sc. Sc2tog. 1 sc in each of next 4 sc. Join with sl st in first sc. 42 sts.

13th to 16th rnds: Ch 1. 1 sc in same sp as last sl st and each st around. Join with sl st in first sc.

17th rnd: Ch 1. 1 sc in same sp as last sl st. *Sc2tog. 1 sc in each of next 4 sc. Rep from * to last 5 sc. Sc2tog. 1 sc in each of next 3 sc. Join with sl st in first sc. 35 sts.

18th to 21st rnds: Ch 1. 1 sc in same sp as last sl st and each sc around. Join with sl st in first sc.

22nd rnd: Ch 1. 1 sc in same sp as last sl st. *Sc2tog. 1 sc in each of next 3 sc. Rep from * to last 4 sc. Sc2tog. 1 sc in each of next 2 sc. Join with sl st in first sc. 28 sts.

23rd to 26th rnds: Ch 1. 1 sc in same sp as last sl st and each sc around. Join with sl st in first sc. Fasten off.

Head

Work from ** to ** as given for Body.

8th rnd: Ch 1. 1 sc in same sp as last sl st. *2 sc in next sc. 1 sc in each of next 6 sc. Rep from * to last 6 sc. 2 sc in next sc. 1 sc in each of next 5 sc. Join with sl st in first sc. 56 sc.

9th rnd: Ch 1. 1 sc in same sp as last sl st. *2 sc in next sc. 1 sc in each of next 7 sc. Rep from * to last 7 sc. 2 sc in next sc. 1 sc in each of next 6 sc. Join with sl st in first sc. 63 sc.

10th rnd: Ch 1. 1 sc in same sp as last sl st. *2 sc in next sc.

1 sc in each of next 8 sc. Rep from * to last 8 sc. 2 sc in next sc. 1 sc in each of next 7 sc. Join with sl st in first sc. 70 sc.

11th rnd: Ch 1. 1 sc in same sp as last sl st. *2 sc in next sc. 1 sc in each of next 9 sc. Rep from * to last 9 sc. 2 sc in next sc. 1 sc in each of next 8 sc. Join with sl st in first sc. 77 sc.

12th to 16th rnds: Ch 1. 1 sc in same sp as last sl st and each sc around. Join with sl st in first sc.

17th rnd: Ch 1. 1 sc in same sp as last sl st. *Sc2tog. 1 sc in each of next 9 sc. Rep from * to last 10 sc. Sc2tog. 1 sc in each of next 8 sc. Join with sl st in first sc. 70 sts.

18th rnd: Ch 1. 1 sc in same sp as last sl st. 1 sc in each of next 4 sc. *Sc2tog. 1 sc in each of next 8 sc. Rep from * to last 5 sc. Sc2tog. 1 sc in each of next 3 sc. Join with sl st in first sc. 63 sts.

19th rnd: Ch 1. 1 sc in same sp as last sl st. *Sc2tog. 1 sc in each of next 7 sts. Rep from * to last 8 sts. Sc2tog. 1 sc in each of next 6 sts. Join with sl st in first sc. 56 sts.

20th rnd: Ch 1. 1 sc in same sp as last sl st. 1 sc in each of next 3 sts. *Sc2tog. 1 sc in each of next 6 sts. Rep from * to last 4 sts. Sc2tog. 1 sc in each of next 2 sc. Join with sl st in first sc. 49 sts.

21st rnd: Ch 1. 1 sc in same sp as last sl st. *Sc2tog. 1 sc in each of next 5 sts. Rep from * to last 6 sts. Sc2tog. 1 sc in each of next 4 sts. Join with sl st in first sc. 42 sts.

22nd rnd: Ch 1. 1 sc in same sp as last sl st. 1 sc in each of next 2 sts. *Sc2tog. 1 sc in each of next 4 sts. Rep from * to last 3 sts. Sc2tog. 1 sc in last sc. Join with sl st in first sc. 35 sts.

23rd rnd: Ch 1. 1 sc in same sp as last sl st. *Sc2tog. 1 sc in each of next 3 sts. Rep from * to last 4 sts. Sc2tog. 1 sc in each of next 2 sts. Join with sl st in first sc. 28 sts.

24th rnd: Ch 1. 1 sc in same sp as last sl st. 1 sc in next st. *Sc2tog. 1 sc in each of next 2 sts. Rep from * to last 2 sts. Sc2tog. Join with sl st in first sc. 21 sts. Fasten off.

Arms (make 2)

With A, ch 2.

1st rnd: 6 sc in 2nd ch from hook. Join with sl st in first sc.

2nd rnd: Ch 1. 2 sc in each sc around. Join with sl st in first sc. 12 sc.

3rd rnd: Ch 1. 1 sc in same sp as last sl st and each sc around. Join with sl st in first sc.

Rep last rnd twice more, joining MC at end of last rnd. With MC, rep last rnd 12 times more. Fasten off.

Ears (make 2)

With MC, ch 2.

1st rnd: 7 sc in 2nd ch from hook. Join with sl st in first sc.

2nd rnd: Ch 1. 2 sc in each sc around. Join with sl st in first sc. 14 sc.

3rd rnd: Ch 1. 1 sc in same sp as last sl st. *2 sc in next sc. 1 sc in next sc. Rep from * to last sc. 2 sc in next sc. Join with sl st in first sc. 21 sc.

4th rnd: Ch 1. 1 sc in same sp as last sl st and each sc around. Join with sl st in first sc. Rep last rnd 13 times more. Fasten off.

Ear Inserts (make 2)

With D, ch 10.

1st row: 1 sc in 2nd ch from hook. 1 sc in each ch to last ch. 3 sc in last ch. Do *not* turn. Working in opposite side of ch, proceed as follows: 1 sc in each rem loop to end of ch.

Fasten off.

Sew Inserts to Ears as illustrated.

Legs (make 2)

With A, ch 2.

1st rnd: 8 sc in 2nd ch from hook. Join with sl st in first sc.

2nd rnd: Ch 1. 2 sc in each sc around. Join with sl st in first sc. 16 sc.

3rd rnd: Ch 1. 1 sc in same sp as last sl st. 1 sc in each sc around. Join with sl st in first sc. Rep last rnd twice more, joining MC at end of last rnd. With MC, rep last rnd 11 times more. Fasten off.

Tail

With MC, ch 2.

1st rnd: 6 sc in 2nd ch from hook. Join with sl st in first sc.

2nd rnd: Ch 1. 2 sc in each sc around. Join with sl st in first sc. 12 sc.

3rd rnd: Ch 1. 1 sc in same sp as last sl st. *2 sc in next sc. 1 sc in next sc. Rep from * to last sc. 2 sc in next sc. Join with sl st in first sc. 18 sc.

4th to 6th rnds: Ch 1. 1 sc in same sp as last sl st and each sc around. Join with sl st in first sc.

7th rnd: Ch 1. *Sc2tog. Rep from * around. Fasten off.

Cheeks

With MC, ch 2.

1st row: 2 sc in 2nd ch from hook. Ch 1. Turn.

2nd row: 2 sc in first sc. 2 sc in next sc. Ch 1. Turn. 4 sc.

3rd row: 2 sc in first sc. 1 sc in each of next 2 sc. 2 sc in last sc. Ch 1. Turn. 6 sc.

4th row: 1 sc in each sc to end of row. Ch 1. Turn.

5th row: Sc2tog. 1 sc in each of next 2 sc. Sc2tog. Ch 1. Turn. 4 sts.

6th row: (Sc2tog) twice. Turn. Rep 2nd to 6th rows once more. Fasten off.

Nose

With E, ch 2.

1st rnd: 6 sc in 2nd ch from hook. Join with sl st to first sc. Fasten off.

FINISHING

Stuff Body, Head, Arms, Legs and sew tog as illustrated. Sew Cheeks in position, placing stuffing as you sew. Sew on Nose. With E and F, embroider Eyes. With D embroider Mouth. Cut 2 strands of E and 1 strand of MC 7"/18cm long and thread through Cheeks for whiskers. Stuff Tail and sew in position.

Carrot

With B, ch 2.

1st rnd: 8 sc in 2nd ch from hook. Join with sl st in first sc.

2nd rnd: Ch 1. 2 sc in each sc around. Join with sl st in first sc. 16 sc.

3rd and 4th rnds: Ch 1. 1 sc in same sp as last sl st. 1 sc in each sc around. Join with sl st in first sc.

5th rnd: Ch 1. 1 sc in same sp as last sl st. (Sc2tog. 1 sc in each of next 3 sc) 3 times. Join with sl st in first sc. 13 sts.

6th and 7th rnds: Ch 1. 1 sc in same sp as last sl st. 1 sc in each st around. Join with sl st in first sc.

8th rnd: Ch 1. 1 sc in same sp as last sl st. (Sc2tog. 1 sc in each of next 2 sc) 3 times. Join with sl st in first sc. 10 sts.

9th to 11th rnds: Ch 1. 1 sc in same sp as last sl st and each st around. Join with sl st in first sc.

12th rnd: Ch 1. 1 sc in same sp as last sl st. (Sc2tog. 1 sc in next sc) 3 times. Join with sl st in first sc. 7 sc.

13th rnd: Ch 1. 1 sc in same sp as last sl st and each st around. Join with sl st in first sc.

14th rnd: Ch 1. 1 sc in same sp as last sl st. (Sc2tog) 3 times. Join with sl st in first sc. 4 sts. Fasten off.

Leaves (make 3).

With C, ch 12.

1st row: 1 sc in 2nd ch from hook. 1 sc in each of next 3 ch. 1 hdc in each of next 3 ch. 1 dc in each of last 4 ch. Fasten off. Sew on Leaves to top of Carrot. Sew Carrot to arm as illustrated.

Necktie

With A, ch 4.

1st row: 4 dc in 4th ch from hook. Turn. 5 dc.

2nd row: Ch 3 (counts as dc). 1 dc in first dc. 1 dc in each of next 3 dc. 2 dc in last dc. Turn. 7 dc.

3rd row: Ch 3 (counts as dc). Miss next dc. 1 dc in each of next 3 dc. Miss next dc. 1 dc in last dc. Ch 2. Turn. 5 dc.

4th row: Ch 2. 1 hdc in each dc to end of row. Turn.

5th row: Ch 2. 1 hdc in each hdc to end of row. Turn. Rep last row until work from beg measures 10"/25.5cm. Fasten off. Knot Necktie around neck.•

BABY'S KITTY BUDDY

Intermediate

MATERIALS

Yarn

Lily® Sugar'n Cream, 2½oz/71g skeins, each approx 120yd/109m (cotton)

- 1 skein each in #00026 Light Blue (MC), #00010 Yellow (A), #00001 White (B), and #00082 Jute (D)
- Small amounts in #00002 Black (C) and #01223 Mod Green (E) for embroidery

Hook

- Size E/4 (3.5mm) crochet hook, *or size needed to obtain gauge*

Notions

- 1 pipe cleaner for Tail
- Stuffing

GAUGE

16 sc and 20 rows = 4"/10cm using size E/4 (3.5mm) hook. *TAKE TIME TO CHECK GAUGE.*

Body

With MC, ch 2.

****1st rnd:** 7 sc in 2nd ch from hook. Join with sl st in first sc.

2nd rnd: Ch 1. 2 sc in each sc around. Join with sl st in first sc. 14 sc.

3rd rnd: Ch 1. 1 sc in same sp as last sl st. *2 sc in next sc. 1 sc in next sc. Rep from * to last sc. 2 sc in next sc. Join with sl st in first sc. 21 sc.

4th rnd: Ch 1. 1 sc in same sp as last sl st. *2 sc in next sc. 1 sc in each of next 2 sc. Rep from * to last 2 sc. 2 sc in next sc. 1 sc in next sc. Join with sl st in first sc. 28 sc.

5th rnd: Ch 1. 1 sc in same sp as last sl st. *2 sc in next sc. 1 sc in each of next 3 sc. Rep from * to last 3 sc. 2 sc in next sc. 1 sc in each of next 2 sc. Join with sl st in first sc. 35 sc.

6th rnd: Ch 1. 1 sc in same sp as last sl st. *2 sc in next sc. 1 sc in each of next 4 sc. Rep from * to last 4 sc. 2 sc in next sc. 1 sc in each of next 3 sc. Join A with sl st in first sc. 42 sc.

7th rnd: With A, ch 1. 1 sc in same sp as last sl st. *2 sc in next sc. 1 sc in each of next 5 sc. Rep from * to last 5 sc. 2 sc in next sc. 1 sc in each of next 4 sc. Join with sl st in first sc. 49 sc.**

8th and 9th rnds: Ch 1. 1 sc in same sp as last sl st and each sc around. Join MC with sl st in first sc at end of 9th rnd.

10th and 11th rnds: With MC, ch 1. 1 sc in same sp as last sl st and each sc around. Join with sl st in first sc.

12th rnd: Ch 1. 1 sc in same sp as last sl st. *Draw up a loop in each of next 2 sc. Yoh and draw through 3 loops on hook—Sc2tog made. 1 sc in each of next 5 sc. Rep from * to last 6 sc. Sc2tog. 1 sc in each of next 4 sc. Join A with sl st in first sc. 42 sts.

13th to 15th rnds: With A, ch 1. 1 sc in same sp as last sl st and each st around. Join MC with sl st in first sc at end of 15th rnd.

16th rnd: With MC, ch 1. 1 sc in same sp as last sl st and each sc around. Join with sl st in first sc.

17th rnd: Ch 1. 1 sc in same sp as last sl st. *Sc2tog. 1 sc in each of next 4 sc. Rep from * to last 5 sc. Sc2tog. 1 sc in each of next 3 sc. Join with sl st in first sc. 35 sts.

18th rnd: Ch 1. 1 sc in same sp as last sl st and each st around. Join A with sl st in first sc.

19th to 21st rnds: With A, ch 1. 1 sc in same sp as last sl st and each sc around. Join MC with sl st in first sc at end of 21st rnd.

22nd rnd: With MC, ch 1. 1 sc in same sp as last sl st. *Sc2tog. 1 sc in each of next 3 sc. Rep from * to last 4 sc. Sc2tog. 1 sc in each of next 2 sc. Join with sl st in first sc. 28 sts.

23rd and 24th rnds: Ch 1. 1 sc in same sp as last sl st and each st around. Join A with sl st in first sc at end of 24th rnd.

25th and 26th rnds: With A, ch 1. 1 sc in same sp as last sl st and each sc around. Join with sl st in first sc. Fasten off

HEAD

With B only, work from ** to ** as given for Body.

8th rnd: Ch 1. 1 sc in same sp as last sl st and each sc around. Join with sl st in first sc.

9th rnd: Ch 1. 1 sc in same sp as last sl st. *2 sc in next sc. 1 sc in each of next 6 sc. Rep from * to last 6 sc. 2 sc in next sc. 1 sc in each of next 5 sc. Join with sl st in first sc. 56 sc.

10th rnd: Ch 1. 1 sc in same sp as last sl st and each sc around. Join with sl st in first sc.

11th rnd: Ch 1. 1 sc in same sp as last sl st. *2 sc in next sc. 1 sc in each of next 7 sc. Rep from * to last 7 sc. 2 sc in next sc. 1 sc in each of next 6 sc. Join with sl st in first sc. 63 sc.

12th to 17th rnds: Ch 1. 1 sc in same sp as last sl st and each sc around. Join with sl st in first sc.

18th rnd: Ch 1. 1 sc in same sp as last sl st. *Sc2tog. 1 sc in each of next 7 sc. Rep from * to last 8 sc. Sc2tog. 1 sc in each of next 6 sc. Join with sl st in first sc. 56 sts.

19th rnd: Ch 1. 1 sc in same sp as last sl st and each st around. Join with sl st in first sc.

20th rnd: Ch 1. 1 sc in same sp as last sl st. 1 sc in each of next 3 sc. *Sc2tog. 1 sc in each of next 6 sc. Rep from * to last 4 sc. Sc2tog. 1 sc in each of next 2 sc. Join with sl st in first sc. 49 sts.

21st rnd: Ch 1. 1 sc in same sp as last sl st. *Sc2tog. 1 sc in each of next 5 sts. Rep from * to last 6 sts. Sc2tog. 1 sc in each of next 4 sts. Join with sl st in first sc. 42 sts.

22nd rnd: Ch 1. 1 sc in same sp as last sl st. 1 sc in each of next 2 sts. *Sc2tog. 1 sc in each of next 4 sts. Rep from * to last 3 sts. Sc2tog. 1 sc in last st. Join with sl st in first sc. 35 sts.

23rd rnd: Ch 1. 1 sc in same sp as last sl st. *Sc2tog. 1 sc in each of next 3 sts. Rep from * to last 4 sts. Sc2tog. 1 sc in each of next 2 sts. Join with sl st in first sc. 28 sts.

24th rnd: Ch 1. 1 sc in same sp as last sl st. 1 sc in next st. *Sc2tog over next 2 sts. 1 sc in each of next 2 sts. Rep from * to last 2 sts. Sc2tog over last 2 sts. Join with sl st in first sc. 21 sts. Fasten off.

Arms (make 2)

With B, ch 2.

1st rnd: 6 sc in 2nd ch from hook. Join with sl st in first sc.

2nd rnd: Ch 1. 2 sc in each sc around. Join with sl st in first sc. 12 sc.

3rd rnd: Ch 1. 1 sc in same sp as last sl st and each sc around. Join

with sl st in first sc.
Rep last rnd twice more, joining MC at end of last rnd. With MC, rep last rnd 12 times more. Fasten off.

Legs (make 2)
With B, ch 2
1st rnd: 8 sc in 2nd ch from hook. Join with sl st in first sc.
2nd rnd: Ch 1. 2 sc in each sc around. Join with sl st in first sc. 16 sc.
3rd rnd: Ch 1. 1 sc in same sp as last sl st and each sc around. Join with sl st in first sc. Rep last rnd twice more, joining MC at end of last rnd. With MC, rep last rnd 11 times more. Fasten off.

Ears (make 2)
With B, ch 2.
1st rnd: 6 sc in 2nd ch from hook. Join with sl st in first sc.
2nd rnd: Ch 1. 1 sc in each sc around. Join with sl st in first sc.
3rd rnd: Ch 1. 2 sc in each sc around. Join with sl st in first sc. 12 sc.
4th rnd: As 2nd rnd.
5th rnd: Ch 1. 1 sc in same sp as last sl st. *2 sc in next sc. 1 sc in next sc. Rep from * to last sc. 2 sc in last sc. Join with sl st in first sc. 18 sc.
6th rnd: As 2nd rnd. Fasten off.

Tail
With B, ch 2.
1st rnd: 6 sc in 2nd ch from hook. Join with sl st in first sc.
2nd and 3rd rnds: Ch 1. 1 sc in each sc around. Join MC with sl st in first sc at end of 3rd rnd.
4th to 6th rnds: With MC, as 2nd rnd. Join A with sl st in first st at end of 6th rnd.
7th to 9th rnds: With A, as 2nd rnd.
Rep last 6 rnds 3 times more, then 4th to 6th rnds once more. Fasten off.

Cheeks
With B, ch 2.
1st row: 2 sc in 2nd ch from hook. Turn.
2nd row: Ch 1. 2 sc in first sc. 2 sc in next sc. Turn. 4 sc.
3rd row: Ch 1. 2 sc in first sc. 1 sc in each of next 2 sc. 2 sc in last sc. Turn. 6 sc.
4th row: Ch 1. 1 sc in each sc to end of row. Turn.
5th row: Ch 1. Sc2tog. 1 sc in each of next 2 sc. Sc2tog. Turn. 4 sts.
6th row: Ch 1. (Sc2tog) twice.

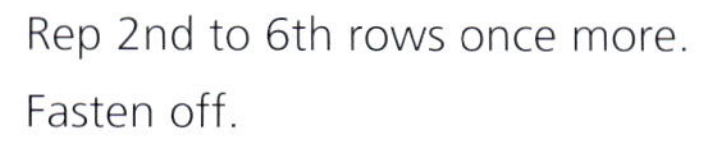

Rep 2nd to 6th rows once more. Fasten off.

Nose
With C, ch 2.
1st rnd: 6 sc in 2nd ch from hook. Join with sl st to first sc. Fasten off.

FINISHING
Stuff Body, Head, Arms, Legs and sew tog as illustrated. Sew Cheeks in position, placing stuffing as you sew. Sew on Nose. With C and E, embroider eyes and mouth. Cut 3 strands of C, 7"/18cm long and thread through Cheeks for whiskers. Insert pipe cleaner into Tail, shape it and sew at bottom back of Body.

Mouse
With D, ch 2.
1st rnd: 8 sc in 2nd ch from hook. Join with sl st in first sc.
2nd rnd: Ch 1. 2 sc in each sc around. Join with sl st in first sc. 16 sc.
3rd and 4th rnds: Ch 1. 1 sc in same sp as last sl st and each sc around. Join with sl st in first sc.
5th rnd: Ch 1. 1 sc in same sp as last sl st. (Sc2tog. 1 sc in each of next 3 sc) 3 times. Join with sl st in first sc. 13 sts.
6th and 7th rnds: Ch 1. 1 sc in same sp as last sl st and each sc around. Join with sl st in first sc.
8th rnd: Ch 1. 1 sc in same sp as last sl st. (Sc2tog. 1 sc in each of next 2 sc) 3 times. Join with sl st in first sc. 10 sts.
9th rnd: Ch 1. 1 sc in same sp as last sl st and each st around. Join with sl st in first sc.
10th rnd: Ch 1. 1 sc in same sp as last sl st. 1sc in each of next 2 sc. Working in front loops only: 3 dc in next sc. Sl st in next sc. 3 dc in next sc. Working through both loops, 1 sc in each of next 4 sc. Join with sl st in first sc.
11th rnd: Ch 1. 1 sc in same sp as last sl st. 1 sc in each of next 2 sc. Working in back loops of 9th rnd only: 1 hdc in each of next 3 sc. 1 sc in each sc of 10th rnd to end of rnd. Join with sl st in first sc.
12th rnd: Ch 1. 1 sc in same sp as last sl st. (Sc2tog. 1 sc in next sc) 3 times. Join with sl st in first sc. 7 sc.
13th rnd: Ch 1. 1 sc in same sp as last sl st and each sc around. Join with sl st in first sc.
14th rnd: Ch 1. 1 sc in same sp as last sl st. (Sc2tog) 3 times. Join with sl st in first sc. 4 sc. Fasten off.

Tail
With D, ch 30. Fasten off. Sew to Mouse.•

HIPPITY-HOP BUNNY HOODIE

Easy

SIZES

6 (12, 18, 24) months.

MEASUREMENTS

Chest 18 (19½, 21½, 23)"/45.5 (49.5, 54.5, 58.5)cm

MATERIALS

Yarn

Bernat® Pipsqueak™, 3½oz/100g skeins, each approx 101yd/92m (polyester)

- 3 (3, 4, 4) skeins in #59005 Whitey White (MC)
- 2 skeins in #59745 Blue Ice (A)

Hook

- Size J/10 (6mm) crochet hook, *or size needed to obtain gauge*

GAUGE

8 sts and 11 rows = 4"/10cm in pat using size J/10 (6mm) hook.

TAKE TIME TO CHECK GAUGE.

HOODIE

Back

**With MC, ch 20 (22, 24, 26).

*****1st row (RS):** 1 sc in 2nd ch from hook. *Ch 1. Skip next ch. 1 sc in next ch. Rep from * to end of chain. Turn. 19 (21, 23, 25) sts.

2nd row: Ch 1. 1 sc in first sc. 1 sc in next ch-1 sp. *Ch 1. Skip next sc. 1 sc in next ch-1 sp. Rep from * to last sc. 1 sc in last sc. Turn.

3rd row: Ch 1. 1 sc in first sc. *Ch 1. Skip next sc. 1 sc in next ch-1 sp. Rep from * to last 2 sc. Ch 1. Skip next sc. 1 sc in last sc. Turn.***

Last 2 rows form pat.

Cont in pat until work from beg measures 7½ (8, 8¾, 9½)"/19 (20.5, 22, 23.5)cm, ending on a WS row.

Shape armholes

Next 2 rows (RS): Ch 1. Sc2tog. Pat to last 2 sts. Sc2tog. Turn. 15 (17, 19, 21) sts rem.**

Cont even in pat until armholes measure 4½ (5, 5½, 5½)"/11.5 (12.5, 14, 14)cm. Fasten off.

Front

Work from ** to ** as given for Back.

Cont even in pat until armhole measures 1 (1½, 1½, 2)"/2.5 (4, 4, 5)cm, ending on a WS row.

Front opening (left side)

1st row (RS): Pat across 7 (8, 9, 10) sts. Turn. Leave rem sts unworked.

Cont even in pat until front opening measures 1½ (1½, 2, 2)"/4 (4, 5, 5)cm, ending on a WS row.

Shape neck

1st row (RS): Ch 1. Pat to last 2 sts. Sc2tog. Turn. 6 (7, 8, 9) sts rem.

2nd row: Ch 1. Sc2tog. Pat to end of row. Turn. 5 (6, 7, 8) sts rem.

3rd row: As 1st row. 4 (5, 6, 7) sts rem.

Cont even in pat until armhole measures same length as Back to shoulder, ending on a WS row. Fasten off.

Front opening (right side)

With RS facing, skip next st. Join yarn with sl st to next st. Ch 1. Pat to end of row. Turn. 7 (8, 9, 10) sts.

Cont even in pat until front opening measures 1½ (1½, 2, 2)"/4 (4, 5, 5)cm, ending on a WS row.

Shape neck

1st row (RS): Ch 1. Sc2tog. Pat to end of row. Turn. 6 (7, 8, 9) sts rem.

2nd row: Ch 1. Pat to last 2 sts. Sc2tog. Turn. 5 (6, 7, 8) sts rem.
3rd row: As 1st row. 4 (5, 6, 7) sts rem.
Cont even in pat until armhole measures same length as Back to shoulder, ending on a WS row. Fasten off.

Sleeves
With MC, ch 14 (14, 16, 16).
Work from *** to *** as given for Back. 13 (13 ,15, 15) sts.
Next (inc) row (WS): 2 sc in first st. Pat to last st. 2 sc in last st. Ch 1. Turn. 15 (15, 17, 17) sts.
Work 2 rows even in pat, taking inc sts into pat.
Rep last 3 rows 2 (3, 3, 3) times more. 19 (21, 23, 23) sts.
Cont even in pat until work from beg measures 6½ (7½, 8½, 9½)"/16.5 (19, 21.5, 24)cm, ending on a WS row.

Shape top
Next 2 rows: Ch 1. Sc2tog. Pat to last 2 sts. Sc2tog. Turn. 15 (17, 19, 19) sts rem. Fasten off.

Hood
With MC, ch 38 (38, 40, 42).
Work from *** to *** as given for Back, then rep 2nd row once. 37 (37, 39, 41) sts.
Next row (RS): Ch 1. Sc2tog. Pat to last 2 sts. Sc2tog. Turn. 35 (35, 37, 39) sts rem.
Work 1 row even in pat.
Rep last 2 rows twice more. 31 (31, 33, 35) sts rem.
Cont even in pat until work from beg measures 8½"/21.5cm, ending on a WS row. Fasten off. Fold Hood in half and sew last row for back seam.

Hood lining
With A, work as given for Hood.
With WS tog, sew Hood and Hood Lining along foundation edge.

Ears (make 2)
With MC, ch 10. Work from *** to *** as given for Back. 9 sts.
Work even in pat until work from beg measures 5 (5½, 5½, 6)"/12.5 (14, 14, 15)cm, ending on a WS row.
Next row: Ch 1. Sc2tog. Pat to last 2 sts. Sc2tog. Turn. 7 sts rem.
Work 3 row even in pat.
Rep last 4 rows twice more. 3 sts rem.
Next row: Ch 1. Sc3tog. Fasten off.

Ear linings (make 2)
With A, work as given for Ears.

With WS tog, sew Ears and Ear Lining along sides. Sew Ears to Hood as shown in picture

FINISHING
Pin garment pieces to measurements and cover with a damp cloth and allow cloth to dry.
Sew shoulder seams. Pin shaped edge of Hood to neck opening, beg at center of front neck edge and matching back seam of Hood to center back neck edge. Sew in Sleeves. Sew side and sleeve seams.

Pompom
With A, wind yarn around 4 fingers approx 50 times. Remove from fingers and tie tightly in center. Cut through each side of loops. Trim to a smooth round shape. Sew securely to Back as shown in picture.•

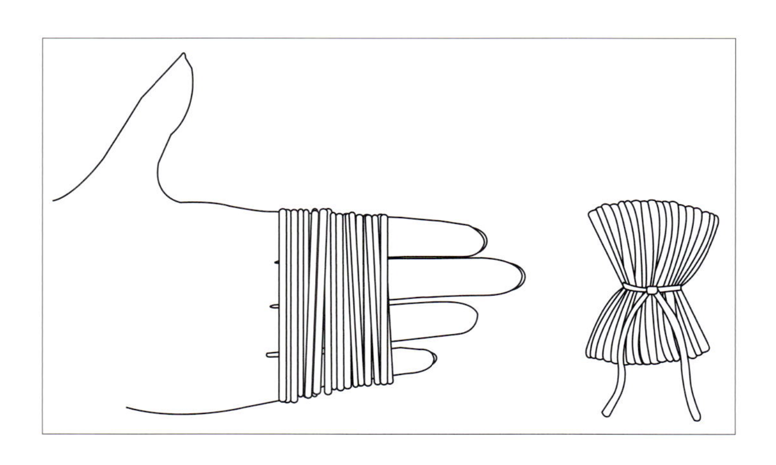

PURRRFECT PLAY RUG

Easy

MEASUREMENTS

Approx 35"/89cm in diameter

MATERIALS

Yarn 

Bernat® Baby Blanket™, 10½oz/300g skeins, each approx 220yds/201m (polyester)

- 4 skeins in #04010 Baby Sand (MC)

Bernat® Baby Blanket™, 3½oz/100g skeins, each approx 72yds/65m (polyester)

- 1 skein each in #03008 Vanilla (A) and #03200 Baby Pink (B)

Hooks

- Size N/15 (10mm) and L/11 (8mm) crochet hooks, *or size needed to obtain gauge*

GAUGE

6 dc and 4 rows = 4"/10 cm with yarn held double and using larger hook. *TAKE TIME TO CHECK GAUGE.*

NOTE

Ch 3 at beg of rnd counts as dc.

RUG

Face

With 2 strands of MC held tog and larger hook, ch 4. Join with sl st to first ch to form ring.

1st rnd: Ch 3. 11 dc in ring. Join with wl st to top of ch 3. 12 dc.

2nd rnd: Ch 3. 1 dc in first dc. 2 dc in each dc around. Join with sl st to top of ch 3. 24 dc.

3rd rnd: Ch 3. 1 dc in first dc. 1 dc in next dc. *2 dc in next dc. 1 dc in next dc. Rep from * around. Join with sl st to top of ch 3. 36 dc.

4th rnd: Ch 3. 1 dc in first dc. 1 dc in each of next 2 dc. *2 dc in next dc. 1 dc in each of next 2 dc. Rep from * around. Join with sl st to top of ch 3. 48 dc.

5th rnd: Ch 3. 1 dc in first dc. 1 dc in each of next 3 dc. *2 dc in next dc. 1 dc in each of next 3 dc. Rep from * around. Join with sl st to top of ch 3. 60 dc.

6th rnd: Ch 3. 1 dc in first dc. 1 dc in each of next 4 dc. *2 dc in next dc. 1 dc in each of next 4 dc. Rep from * around. Join with sl st to top of ch 3. 72 dc.

7th rnd: Ch 3. 1 dc in first dc. 1 dc in each of next 5 dc. *2 dc in next dc. 1 dc in each of next 5 dc. Rep from * around. Join with sl st to top of ch 3. 84 dc.

8th rnd: Ch 3. 1 dc in first dc. 1 dc in each of next 6 dc. *2 dc in next dc. 1 dc in each of next 6 dc. Rep from * around. Join with sl st to top of ch 3. 96 dc.

9th rnd: Ch 3. 1 dc in first dc. 1 dc in each of next 7 dc. *2 dc in next dc. 1 dc in each of next 7 dc. Rep from * around. Join with sl st to top of ch 3. 108 dc.

Cont as established, inc 12 dc every rnd until piece measures approx 35"/89cm in diameter. Fasten off.

PURRRFECT PLAY RUG

Ears (make 2)

With 2 strands of MC held tog and larger hook, ch 18.

1st row: 1 sc in 2nd ch from hook. 1 sc in each ch to end of chain. Turn. 17 sc.

2nd row: Ch 1. 1 sc in each sc to end of row. Turn.

3rd row: Ch 1. Sc2tog. 1 sc in each sc to last 2 sc. Sc2tog. Turn. 15 sts.

4th row: Ch 1. 1 sc in each st to end of row. Turn.

Rep last 2 rows to 3 sts.

Next row: Ch 1. Sc3tog. Fasten off

Inner ears (make 2)

With 1 strand of B and smaller hook, ch 14.

1st row: 1 sc in 2nd ch from hook. 1 sc in each ch to end of chain. Turn. 13 sc.

2nd row: Ch 1. Sc2tog. 1 sc in each sc to last 2 sc. Sc2tog. 11 sts.

3rd row: Ch 1. 1 sc in each st to end of row. Turn.

Rep last 2 rows to 3 sts.

Next row: Ch 1. Sc3tog. Fasten off.

Sew Inner Ear to Ear as shown in picture.

Eyes (make 2)

With 1 strand of A and smaller hook, ch 4.

****1st rnd:** 9 dc in 4th ch from hook. Join with sl st to top of ch 3. 10 dc.

2nd rnd: Ch 3 (counts as dc). 1 dc in first dc (counts as 2 dc). 2 dc in each dc around. Join with sl st to top of ch 3. 20 dc.**

3rd rnd: Ch 3 (counts as dc). 1 dc in first dc (counts as 2 dc). 1 dc in next dc. *2 dc in next dc. 1 dc in next dc. Rep from * around. Join with sl st to top of ch 3. 30 dc. Fasten off.

Pupils (make 2)

With 1 strand of MC and smaller hook, ch 4. Work from ** to ** as given for Eye. Fasten off. Sew Pupil to Eye as shown in picture.

Nose

With 1 strand of B and smaller hook, ch 9.

1st row (RS): 1 sc in 2nd ch from hook. 1 sc in each ch to end of chain. Turn. 8 sc.

2nd row: Ch 1. Sc2tog. 1 sc in each sc to last 2 sc. Sc2tog. Turn. 6 sts.

3rd row: As 2nd row. 4 sts.

4th row: Ch 1. (Sc2tog) twice. 2 sts.

5th row: Ch 1. Sc2tog. Do not fasten off.

Ch 1. Work 1 rnd of sc around 3 edges, working 3 sc in each corner. Join with sl st to first sc. Fasten off.

FINISHING

Sew Eyes, Nose and Ears to Face as shown in picture.

Mouth

With 2 strands of A and smaller hook, ch 30. Fasten off.

With 2 strands of A and smaller hook, ch 15. Fasten off

Sew longer chain to Face, starting at tip of Nose and curving up to form Mouth. Sew shorter chain to form other side of Mouth.

Whiskers (make 4)

With 2 strands of A and smaller hook, ch 12. Fasten off.

Sew 2 Whiskers on either side of face as shown in picture.•

FRANCIS THE FOX

Intermediate

MEASUREMENTS

Total Height Approx 22"/56cm

MATERIALS

Yarn

Caron® Simply Soft™, 6oz/170g skeins, each approx 315yd/288m (acrylic) (4)

- 2 skeins in #39765 Pumpkin (A)
- 1 skein in #39771 Chartreuse (C)

Caron® Simply Soft® Heathers™, 5oz/141g skeins, each approx 250yd/229m (acrylic) (4)

- 1 skein in #H9508 Charcoal Heather (B)

Bernat® Pipsqueak™, 3½oz/100g skeins, each approx 101yd/92m (polyester) (5)

- 1 skein in #59005 Whitey White (D)

Hooks

- Sizes E/4 (3.5mm) and I/9 (5.5mm) crochet hooks, *or size needed to obtain gauges*

Notions

- Polyester fiberfill
- Pair of 10 mm Safety Eyes or 2 buttons for Eyes
- Stitch marker

GAUGES

17 sc and 18 rows = 4"/10cm using Caron® Simply Soft™ and smaller hook.

9 sc and 12 rows = 4"/10cm using Bernat® Pipsqueak™ and larger hook.

TAKE TIME TO CHECK GAUGES.

FOX

Body

With A and smaller hook, ch 2.

1st rnd: 8 sc in 2nd ch from hook. Join with sl st to first sc.

2nd rnd: Ch 1. 2 sc in each sc around. Join with sl st to first sc. 16 sc.

3rd rnd: Ch 1. 2 sc in first sc. 1 sc in next sc. *2 sc in next sc. 1 sc in next sc. Rep from * around. Join with sl st to first sc. 24 sc.

4th rnd: Ch 1. 2 sc in first sc. 1 sc in each of next 2 sc. *2 sc in next sc. 1 sc in each of next 2 sc. Rep from * around. Join with sl st to first sc. 32 sc.

5th rnd: Ch 1. 2 sc in first sc. 1 sc in each of next 3 sc. *2 sc in next sc. 1 sc in each of next 3 sc. Rep from * around. Join with sl st to first sc. 40 sc.

6th rnd: Ch 1. 2 sc in first sc. 1 sc in each of next 4 sc. *2 sc in next sc. 1 sc in each of next 4 sc. Rep from * around. Join with sl st to first sc. 48 sc.

7th rnd: Ch 1. 2 sc in first sc. 1 sc in each of next 5 sc. *2 sc in next sc. 1 sc in each of next 5 sc. Rep from * around. Join with sl st to first sc. 56 sc.

8th rnd: Ch 1. 2 sc in first sc. 1 sc in each of next 6 sc. *2 sc in next sc. 1 sc in each of next 6 sc. Rep from * around. Join with sl st to first sc. 64 sc.

9th rnd: Ch 1. 2 sc in first sc. 1 sc in each of next 7 sc. *2 sc in next sc. 1 sc in each of next 7 sc. Rep from * around. Join with sl st to first sc. 72 sc. Place marker on last rnd.

10th rnd: Ch 1. 1 sc in each sc around. Join with sl st to first sc.

Rep last rnd until work from marked rnd measures 5"/12.5cm.

Beg dec rnds

1st rnd: Ch 1. 1 sc in each of first 7 sc. *Sc2tog. 1 sc in each of next 7 sc. Rep from * to last 2 sc. Sc2tog. Join with sl st to first sc. 64 sts.

2nd to 5th rnds: Ch 1. 1 sc in each st around. Join with sl st to first sc.

6th rnd: Ch 1. 1 sc in each of first 6 sc. *Sc2tog. 1 sc in each of next 6 sc. Rep from * to last 2 sc. Sc2tog. Join with sl st to first sc. 56 sts.

7th to 10th rnds: As 2nd to 5th rnds.

11th rnd: Ch 1. 1 sc in each of first 5 sc. *Sc2tog. 1 sc in each of next 5 sc. Rep from * to last 2 sc. Sc2tog. Join with sl st to first sc. 48 sts.

12th to 15th rnds: As 2nd to 5th rnds.

16th rnd: Ch 1. 1 sc in each` of first 4 sc. *Sc2tog. 1 sc in each of next 4 sc. Rep from * to last 2 sc. Sc2tog. Join with sl st to first sc. 40 sts.

17th to 20th rnds: As 2nd to 5th rnds.

21st rnd: Ch 1. 1 sc in each of first 3 sc. *Sc2tog. 1 sc in each of next 3 sc. Rep from * to last 2 sc. Sc2tog. Join with sl st to first sc. 32 sts.

22nd rnd: Ch 1. 1 sc in each st around. Join with sl st to first sc. Fasten off.

Stuff Body

Head

Nose

With B and smaller hook, ch 2.

1st rnd: 8 sc in 2nd ch from hook. Join with sl st to first sc.

2nd rnd: Ch 1. 2 sc in each sc around. Join with sl st to first sc. 16 sc.

3rd and 4th rnds: Ch 1. 1 sc in each sc around. Join A with sl st to first sc.

5th and 6th rnds: With A, ch 1. 1 sc in each sc around. Join with sl st to first sc.

7th rnd: Ch 1. 2 sc in each sc around. Join with sl st to first sc. 32 sc.

8th rnd: Ch 1. 1 sc in each sc around. Join with sl st to first sc.

9th rnd: Ch 1. 1 sc in each of first 3 sc. *2 sc in next sc. 1 sc in each of next 3 sc. Rep from * to last sc. 2 sc in last sc. Join with sl st to first sc. 40 sc.

10th rnd: As 8th rnd.

11th rnd: Ch 1. 1 sc in each of first 4 sc. *2 sc in next sc. 1 sc in each of next 4 sc. Rep from * to last sc. 2 sc in last sc. Join with sl st to first sc. 48 sc.

12th rnd: As 8th rnd.

Cont as established, inc 8 sc evenly spaced across every

other rnd to 64 sc.

Next rnd: Ch 1. 1 sc in each sc around. Join with sl st to first sc.

Rep last rnd 7 times more.

Beg dec rnds

1st rnd: Ch 1. 1 sc in each of first 6 sc. *Sc2tog. 1 sc in each of next 6 sc. Rep from * to last 2 sc. Sc2tog. Join with sl st to first sc. 56 sts.

2nd rnd: Ch 1. 1 sc in each st around. Join with sl st to first sc.

3rd rnd: Ch 1. 1 sc in each of first 5 sc. *Sc2tog. 1 sc in each of next 5 sc. Rep from * to last 2 sc. Sc2tog. Join with sl st to first sc. 48 sts.

4th rnd: As 2nd rnd.

5th rnd: Ch 1. 1 sc in each of first 4 sc. *Sc2tog. 1 sc in each of next 4 sc. Rep from * to last 2 sc. Sc2tog. Join with sl st to first sc. 40 sts.

6th rnd: As 2nd rnd.

7th rnd: Ch 1. 1 sc in each of first 6 sc. *Sc2tog. 1 sc in each of next 6 sc. Rep from * to last 2 sc. Sc2tog. Join with sl st to first sc. 35 sts.

8th rnd: As 2nd rnd.

Stuff Head.

9th rnd: Ch 1. 1 sc in each of first 3 sc. *Sc2tog. 1 sc in each of next 3 sc. Rep from * to last 2 sc. Sc2tog. Join with sl st to first sc. 28 sts.

10th rnd: As 2nd rnd.

11th rnd: Ch 1. 1 sc in each of first 2 sc. *Sc2tog. 1 sc in each of next 2 sc. Rep from * to last 2 sc. Sc2tog. Join with sl st to first sc. 21 sts.

12th rnd: As 2nd rnd.

13th rnd: Ch 1. 1 sc in first sc. *Sc2tog. 1 sc in next sc. Rep from * to last 2 sc. Sc2tog. Join with sl st to first sc. 14 sts.

14th rnd: Ch 1. *Sc2tog. Rep from * around. Join with sl st to first st. 7 sts. Fasten off, leaving a long end. Draw end through rem loops and pull tightly. Fasten securely.

Sew Head to top of Body.

Fuzzy Beard

With D and larger hook, ch 5.

1st row: 1 sc in 2nd ch from hook. 1 sc in each ch to end of chain. Turn. 4 sc.

2nd row: Ch 1. 2 sc in each sc to end of row. Turn. 8 sc.

3rd row: Ch 1. 2 sc in first sc. *1 sc in next sc. 2 sc in next sc. Rep from * to last sc. 1 sc in last sc. 12 sc.

4th row: As 3rd row. 18 sc.

5th row: Ch 1. 2 sc in first sc. *1 sc in each of next 2 sc. 2 sc in next sc. Rep from * to last 2 sc. 1 sc in each of last 2 sc. 24 sc

6th row: Ch 1. 2 sc in first sc. *1 sc in each of next 3 sc. 2 sc in next sc. Rep from * to last 3 sc. 1 sc in each of last 3 sc. 30 sc.

7th row: Ch 1. 2 sc in first sc. *1 sc in each of next 4 sc. 2 sc in next sc. Rep from * to last 4 sc. 1 sc in each of last 4 sc. 36 sc.

Cont as established, inc 6 sc evenly spaced on each of next 4 rows. 60 sc at end of 11th row. Fasten off.

Curve Beard around bottom of Nose, and up sides of Face to create Beard shape as shown in picture.

Attach Safety Eyes or buttons to part of Beard that curves upwards. Sew in position.

With B, embroider mouth.

Outer Ears (make 2)

With smaller hook and A, ch 11.

1st row: 1 sc in 2nd ch from hook. 1 sc in each ch to end of ch. Turn. 10 sc.

2nd to 7th rows: Ch 1. 1 sc in each sc to end of row. Turn.

8th row: Ch 1. Sc2tog. 1 sc in each of next 6 sc. Sc2tog. Turn. 8 sts.

9th row: Ch 1. Sc2tog. 1 sc in each of next 4 sc. Sc2tog. Turn. 6 sts.

10th row: Ch 1. Sc2tog. 1 sc in each of next 2 sc. Sc2tog. Turn. 4 sts.

11th row: Ch 1. (Sc2tog) twice. Turn. 2 sts.

12th row: Ch 1. Sc2tog. Fasten off.

Inner Ears (make 2)

With smaller hook and D, ch 9.

1st row: 1 sc in 2nd ch from hook. 1 sc in each ch to end of ch. Turn. 8 sc.

2nd and 3rd rows: Ch 1. 1 sc in each sc to end of row. Turn.

4th row: Ch 1. Sc2tog. 1 sc in each of next 4 sc. Sc2tog. Turn. 6 sts.

5th row: Ch 1. Sc2tog. 1 sc in each of next 2 sc. Sc2tog. Turn. 4 sts.

6th row: Ch 1. (Sc2tog) twice. Turn. 2 sts.

7th row: Ch 1. Sc2tog. Fasten off.

Holding WS of Outer and Inner Ears tog, with larger hook and 2 strands of A held tog, join with sl st to bottom right corner. Working through both thicknesses, Ch 1. Work 1 row of sc evenly to tip of Ear. Work 3 sc in tip of Ear. Work 1 row of sc evenly along left side edge. Fasten off. Sew Ears to top of Head.

Arms (make 2)

With smaller hook and B, ch 2.

1st rnd: 8 sc in 2nd ch from hook. Join with sl st to first sc.

2nd rnd: Ch 1. 2 sc in each sc around. Join with sl st to first sc. 16 sc.

3rd rnd: Ch 1. 1 sc in each sc around. Join with sl st to first sc.

4th rnd: Ch 1. 1 sc in each of first 3 sc. *2 sc in next sc. 1 sc in each of next 3 sc. Rep from * to last sc. 2 sc in last sc. Join with sl st to first sc. 20 sc.

5th rnd: Ch 1. 1 sc in each sc around.

Rep last rnd 9 times more. Break B, join A.

Next rnd: With A, ch 1. 1 sc in each of first 3 sc. *Sc2tog. 1 sc in each of next 3 sc. Rep from * to last 2 sc. Sc2tog. Join with sl st to first sc. 16 sts.

Next rnd: Ch 1. 1 sc in each st around. Join with sl st to first sc.

Rep last rnd until Arm measures approx 6"/15cm from beg.

Fasten off.

Stuff Arms lightly. Sew Arms to either side of Body.

Legs (make 2)

With smaller hook and B, ch 2.

1st rnd: 8 sc in 2nd ch from hook. Join with sl st to first sc.

2nd rnd: Ch 1. 2 sc in each sc around. Join with sl st to first sc. 16 sc.

3rd rnd: Ch 1. 1 sc in each sc around. Join with sl st to first sc.

4th rnd: Ch 1. 1 sc in first sc. *2 sc in next sc. 1 sc in next sc. Rep from * to last sc. 2 sc in last sc. Join with sl st to first sc. 24 sc.

5th rnd: Ch 1. 1 sc in each sc around. Join with sl st to first sc.

Rep last rnd 9 times more. Break B, join A.

Next rnd: With A, ch 1. 1 sc in each of first 4 sc. *Sc2tog. 1 sc in each of next 4 sc. Rep from * to last 2 sc. Sc2tog. Join with sl st to first sc. 20 sts.

Next 10 rnds: Ch 1. 1 sc in each st around. Join with sl st to first sc.

Next rnd: Ch 1. 1 sc in each of first 3 sc. *Sc2tog. 1 sc in each of next 3 sc. Rep from * to last 2 sc. Sc2tog. Join with sl st to first sc. 16 sts.

Next 10 rnds: Ch 1. 1 sc in each st around. Join with sl st to first sc.

Fasten off.

Stuff Legs lightly. Sew Legs to bottom of Body.

Tail

With 2 strands of A held tog and larger hook, ch 20. Join with sl st to first ch.

1st rnd: Ch 2 (counts as hdc). 1 hdc in each ch around. Join with sl st to top of ch 2. 20 hdc.

2nd rnd: Ch 2 (counts as hdc). 1 hdc in each hdc around. Join with sl st to top of ch 2.

Rep last rnd until Tail from beg measures approx 4"/10cm. Break A. Join 1 strand of D.

Next rnd: With D, ch 2 (counts as hdc). 1 hdc in each hdc around. Join with sl st to top of ch 2.

Next rnd: Ch 2 (counts as hdc). 1 hdc in each of next 2 hdc. Hdc2tog. *1 hdc in each of next 3 hdc. Hdc2tog. Rep from * around. Join with sl st to top of ch 2. 16 sts.

Next rnd: Ch 2 (counts as hdc). 1 hdc in next hdc. Hdc2tog. *1 hdc in each of next 2 hdc. Hdc2tog. Rep from * around. Join with sl st to top of ch 2. 12 sts.

Next rnd: Ch 2 (counts as hdc). *Hdc2tog. 1 hdc in next hdc. Rep from * to last 2 sts. Hdc2tog. Join with sl st to top of ch 2. 8 sts.

Next rnd: (Hdc2tog) 4 times. 4 sts.

Fasten off, leaving a long end. Draw end tightly through rem loops. Fasten securely.

Necktie

With C and smaller hook, ch 6.

1st row: 1 sc in 2nd ch from hook. 1 sc in each ch to end of ch. Turn. 5 sc.

2nd to 7th rows: Ch 1. 1 sc in each sc to end of row. Turn.

8th row: Ch 1. 2 sc in first sc. 1 sc in each sc to last sc. 2 sc in last sc. Turn. 7 sc.

9th row: As 8th row. 9 sc.

10th to 14th rows: Ch 1. 1 sc in each sc to end of row. Turn.

15th to 17th rows: Ch 1. Sc2tog. 1 sc in each sc to last 2 sc. Sc2tog. Turn. 3 sts rem.

18th row: Ch 1. Sc3tog. Fasten off.

Tie 'knot'

With C and smaller hook, ch 7.

1st row: 1 sc in 2nd ch from hook. 1 sc in each ch to end of ch. Turn. 6 sc.

2nd to 13th rows: Ch 1. 1 sc in each sc to end of row. Turn.

Fasten off.

Sew last row and foundation row tog. Place Tie into loop of Tie 'knot' and sew in position. Attach Tie to front of Body as shown in picture.•

BABY KITTY HAT

Easy

SIZE

12–18 months.

MATERIALS

Yarn

Bernat® Softee® Baby™, 5oz/140g skeins, each approx 362yd/331m (acrylic)

- 1 skein in #02002 Pale Blue

Hook

- Size G/6 (4mm) crochet hook, *or size needed to obtain gauge*

Notions

- Stitch marker

GAUGE

16 sc and 19 rows = 4"/10cm using G/6 (4mm) hook.
TAKE TIME TO CHECK GAUGE.

STITCH GLOSSARY

FPhdc Yoh and draw up a loop around post of next hdc from front to back to front. Yoh and draw through all 3 loops on hook.

Hdctbl Half double crochet in back loop only.

Hdctbl2tog (Yoh and draw up a loop in back loop of next stitch) twice. Yoh and draw through all loops on hook.

HAT

Note: Ch 2 at beg of rnd does not count as hdc. Join all rnds with sl st to first st.

Ch 64. Join with sl st to first ch to form a ring.

1st rnd: Ch 3 (counts as dc). 1 dc in each ch around. Join with sl st to top of ch 3. 64 sts.

2nd rnd: Ch 2. 1 hdctbl in each dc around. Join.

3rd rnd: Ch 2. *1 hdctbl in each of next 3 sts. FPhdc around next st. Rep from * around. Join.

Rep 3rd rnd until Hat from beg measures 5"/12.5cm.

Shape Crown

1st rnd: Ch 2. (1 hdctbl in each of next 3 sts. FPhdc around next st. 1 hdctbl in next st. Hdctbl2tog. FPhdc around next st) 8 times around. Join. 56 sts.

2nd rnd: Ch 2. (1 hdctbl in each of next 3 sts. FPhdc around next st. 1 hdctbl in each of next 2 sts. FPhdc around next st) 8 times. Join.

3rd rnd: Ch 2. (1 hdctbl in next st. Hdctbl2tog. FPhdc around next st. 1 hdctbl in each of next 2 sts. FPhdc around next st) 8 times. 48 sts. Join.

4th rnd: Ch 2. (1 hdctbl in each of next 2 sts. FPhdc around next st. 1 hdctbl in each of next 2 sts. FPhdc around next st) 8 times around. Join.

5th rnd: Ch 2. (1 hdctbl in each of next 2 sts. FPhdc around next st. Hdctbl2tog. FPhdc around next st) 8 times. 40 sts. Join.

6th rnd: Ch 2. (Hdctbl2tog. FPhdc around next st. 1 hdctbl around next st. FPhdc around next st) 8 times. 32 sts. Join.

7th rnd: Ch 2. (Skip next hdc. FPhdc around next st) 16 times. 16 sts. Join.

8th rnd: Ch 2. (Hdctbl2tog) 8 times. 8 sts. Join.

Fasten off, leaving a long end.

Draw end tightly through rem sts and fasten securely.

FINISHING

Ears (make 2)

Ch 10.

1st row: 1 sc in 2nd ch from hook and each ch to end of chain. Turn. 9 sc.

2nd to 4th rows: Ch 1. Sc2tog. 1 sc in each st to last 2 sts. Sc2tog. Turn. 3 sts at end of 4th row.

5th row: Ch 1. Sc3tog. Fasten off.

Sew Ears to top of Hat as shown in photo.•

MAMA KANGAROO & JOEY

Easy

MEASUREMENTS

Mama Approx 10"/25.5cm tall, including ears

Joey Approx 5"/12.5cm tall, including ears

MATERIALS

Yarn (4)

Caron® Simply Soft™, 6oz/170g skeins, each approx 315yd/288m (acrylic)

- 1 skein each in #39703 Bone (MC) and #39750 Chocolate

Hook

- Size E/4 (3.5mm) crochet hook, *or size needed for desired gauge*

Notions

- Polyester fiberfill
- Stitch marker

GAUGE

Gauge is not critical for this project. Work tightly, so stuffing will not show through stitches.

NOTES

1) Pieces are worked in continuous rounds, with RS facing throughout. Do *not* turn and do *not* join at the end of rounds. Place a marker to indicate the end of the first round and move the marker up as work progresses.

2) To reduce finishing time, weave in ends as work progresses.

MAMA

Head

Beginning at top of head, with larger hook, ch 2.

Round 1 (RS): Work 6 sc in 2nd ch from hook; do *not* join and do *not* turn—6 sc. Place a marker to indicate the end of the round and move the marker up as each round is completed.

Round 2: Work 2 sc in each sc around—12 sc.

Round 3: [Sc in next sc, 2 sc in next sc] 6 times—18 sc.

Round 4: [Sc in next 2 sc, 2 sc in next sc] 6 times—24 sc.

Round 5: [Sc in next 3 sc, 2 sc in next sc] 6 times—30 sc.

Rounds 6–12: Sc in each sc around.

Round 13: [Sc in next 3 sc, sc2tog] 6 times—24 sc.

Round 14: Sc in each sc around.

Round 15: [Sc in next 2 sc, sc2tog] 6 times—18 sc.

Neck Rounds 16–20: Sc in each sc around.

Body Round 21: [Sc in next 2 sc, 2 sc in next sc] 6 times—24 sc.

Rounds 22–24: Sc in each sc around.

Round 25: [Sc in next 3 sc, 2 sc in next sc] 6 times—30 sc.

Rounds 26–28: Sc in each sc around.

Round 29: [Sc in next 4 sc, 2 sc in next sc] 6 times—36 sc.

Round 30: Sc in each sc around.

Round 31: [Sc in next 5 sc, 2 sc in next sc] 6 times—42 sc.

Round 32: Sc in each sc around.

Round 33: [Sc in next 3 sc, 2 sc in next sc] 10 times, sc in next 2 sc—52 sc.

Rounds 34 and 35: Sc in each sc around.

Round 36: [Sc in next 4 sc, 2 sc in next sc] 10 times, sc in next 2 sc—62 sc.

Rounds 37 and 38: Sc in each sc around.

Round 39: [Sc in next 5 sc, 2 sc in next sc] 10 times, sc in next 2 sc—72 sc.

Rounds 40 and 41: Sc in each sc around.

Round 42: [Sc in next 4 sc, sc2tog] 12 times—60 sc.

Round 43: [Sc in next 3 sc, sc2tog] 12 times—48 sc.

Stuff head and body.

Continue to stuff piece as work progresses.

Round 44: [Sc in next 2 sc, sc2tog] 12 times—36 sc.

Round 45: [Sc in next sc, sc2tog] 12 times—24 sc.

Round 46: [Sc in next sc, sc2tog] 8 times—16 sc.

Round 47: [Sc2tog] 8 times—8 sc. Fasten off, leaving a long tail.

With yarn needle, weave tail through stitches of last round. Pull gently, but firmly, to close opening. Tie securely and weave in end.

Muzzle

Beginning at center front of muzzle, with larger hook, ch 2.

Round 1 (RS): Work 6 sc in 2nd ch from hook; do *not* join and do *not* turn—6 sc. Place a marker to indicate the end of the round and move the marker up as each round is completed.

Round 2: Work 2 sc in each sc around—12 sc.

Rounds 3 and 4: Sc in each sc around.

Round 5: [Sc in next sc, 2 sc in next sc] 6 times—18 sc.

Rounds 6 and 7: Sc in each sc around.

Round 8: [Sc in next 2 sc, 2 sc in next sc] 6 times—24 sc. Fasten off, leaving a long tail for sewing. Stuff muzzle and sew to lower, center front of head.

Ears (make 2)

With larger hook, ch 11.

Row 1: Dc in 4th ch from hook (beginning ch counts as first dc), hdc in next 3 ch, sc in next 3 ch, 3 sc in last ch; rotate piece to work across opposite side of foundation ch (do *not* turn piece over, keep same side facing you), sc in next 3 ch, hdc in next 3 ch, dc in last 2 ch, turn—19 sts.

Row 2: Ch 1, working in back loops only, sc in first 9 sts, 3 sc in next st (at tip), sc in last 9 sts—21 sts.

Fasten off, leaving a long tail for sewing. Sew one ear to each side of head, toward the back.

Arms (make 2)

Beginning at top of arm, with larger hook, ch 2.

Round 1: Work 7 sc in 2nd ch from hook; do *not* join and do *not* turn—7 sc. Place a marker to indicate the end of the round and move the marker up as each round is completed.

Round 2: Work 2 sc in each sc around—14 sc.

Rounds 3–8: Sc in each sc around.

Rounds 9 and 10: Sl st in next 4 sc, hdc in next 6 sc, sl st in next 4 sts.

Round 11: Sc in next 4 sl sts, hdc in next 6 hdc, sc in next 4 sl sts.

Round 12: Sc in next 3 sc, [sc2tog] 4 times, sc in next 3 sc—10 sc.

Round 13: Sc in each sc around.

Stuff piece. Continue to stuff piece as work progresses.

Round 14: Sc in first 3 sc, [sc2tog] 2 times, sc in last 3 sc—8 sc.

Round 15: Sc in each sc around.

Round 16: Sc in first sc, 2 sc in next sc, sc in next 5 sc, 2 sc in last sc—10 sc.

Rounds 17 and 18: Sc in each sc around.

Round 19: [Sc2tog] 5 times—5 sc. Fasten off, leaving a long tail. With yarn needle, weave tail through stitches of last round. Pull gently, but firmly, to close opening. Tie securely. Using remaining long tail, sew one arm to each side of body, below neck.

Legs (make 2)

Beginning at top of leg, with larger hook, ch 2.

Round 1 (RS): Work 8 sc in 2nd ch from hook; do *not* join and do *not* turn—8 sc. Place a marker to indicate the end of the round and move the marker up as each round is completed.

Round 2: Work 2 sc in each sc around—16 sc.

Round 3: [Sc in next sc, 2 sc in next sc] 8 times—24 sc.

Round 4: Sc in each sc around.

Round 5: [Sc in next 2 sc, 2 sc in next sc] 8 times—32 sc.

Rounds 6–10: Sc in each sc around.

Round 11: [Sc in next 2 sc, sc2tog] 8 times—24 sc.

Round 12: Sc in each sc around.

Round 13: [Sc in next sc, sc2tog] 8 times—16 sc.

Rounds 14 and 15: Sc in each sc around.

Round 16: [Sc in next 2 sc, sc2tog] 4 times—12 sc.

Rounds 17 and 18: Sc in each sc around.

Round 19: [Sc in next sc, 2 sc in next sc] 6 times—18 sc.

Rounds 20–23: Sc in each sc around.

Stuff piece lightly. Continue to stuff piece as work progresses.

Round 24: [Sc in next 8 sc, 2 sc in next sc] 2 times—20 sc.

Rounds 25–30: Sc in each sc around.

Round 31: [Sc in next 2 sc, sc2tog] 5 times—15 sc.

Round 32: [Sc in next sc, sc2tog] 5 times—10 sc.

Round 33: [Sc2tog] 5 times—5 sc. Fasten off, leaving a very long tail. With yarn needle, weave tail through stitches of last round. Pull gently, but firmly, to close opening. Tie securely, do *not* cut tail, use tail to shape and sew one leg to each side of body, as follows: Flatten top of leg (widest end) slightly and pin it to the side of the body, below the arm. Fold the leg slightly so the foot is positioned to the floor and tack the foot to the leg. Sew the leg to the body. With yarn needle and another length of yarn, sew 2 lines into each foot to form toes. Weave in ends.

Tail

Beginning at tip of tail, with larger hook, ch 2.

Round 1: Work 6 sc in 2nd ch from hook—6 sc. Place a marker to indicate the end of the round and move the marker up as each round is completed.

Rounds 2–6: Sc in each sc around.

Round 7: [Sc in next 2 sc, 2 sc in next sc] 2 times—8 sc.

Rounds 8–10: Sc in each sc around.

Round 11: [Sc in next 3 sc, 2 sc in next sc] 2 times—10 sc.

Rounds 12–15: Sc in each sc around.

Round 16: [Sc in next 4 sc, 2 sc in next sc] 2 times—12 sc.

Rounds 17 and 18: Sc in each sc around.

Round 19: [Sc in next 5 sc, 2 sc in next sc] 2 times—14 sc.

Stuff piece. Continue to stuff piece as work progresses.

Rounds 20 and 21: Sc in each sc around.

Round 22: [Sc in next 6 sc, 2 sc in next sc] 2 times—16 sc.

Round 23: Sc in each sc around.

Round 24: [Sc in next 4 sc, 2 sc in next sc] 3 times, sc in next sc—19 sc.

Rounds 25 and 26: Sc in each sc around.

Round 27: [Sc in next 5 sc, 2 sc in next sc] 3 times, sc in next sc—22 sc.

Round 28: Sc in each sc around. Fasten off, leaving a long tail for sewing.

With yarn needle, sew tail to bottom back, centered between legs. Weave in end.

Pouch

Beginning at lower edge, with larger hook, ch 29.

Row 1: Working in back bars only, sc in 2nd ch from hook and in each remaining ch across, turn—28 sc.

Row 2: Ch 1, 2 sc in first sc, sc in each sc across to last sc, 2 sc in last sc, turn—30 sc.

Rows 3–19: Ch 1, sc in each sc across, turn. Fasten off, leaving a very long tail for sewing.

With yarn needle, sew sides and bottom of pouch to front of body between legs, gather bottom of pouch to fit.

FINISHING

With yarn needle and brown yarn, using photograph as a guide, embroider straight st eyes on face about ½"/1.5cm tall and about ¾"/2cm apart, above muzzle. Embroider straight st nostrils about ¼"/0.5cm apart and about 1"/2.5cm from end of muzzle. Embroider straight st mouth at end of muzzle.

JOEY

Head

Beginning at top of head, with smaller hook, ch 2.

Round 1 (RS): Work 6 sc in 2nd ch from hook; do *not* join and do *not* turn—6 sc. Place a marker to indicate the end of the round and move the marker up as each round is completed.

Round 2: Work 2 sc in each sc around—12 sc.

Round 3: [Sc in next 2 sc, 2 sc in next sc] 4 times—16 sc.

Rounds 4–6: Sc in each sc around.

Round 7: [Sc in next 2 sc, sc2tog] 4 times—12 sc.

Round 8: [Sc in next sc, sc2tog] 4 times—8 sc.

Neck Rounds 9–10: Sc in each sc around.

Stuff head and neck. Do *not* continue to stuff.

Body Round 11: [Sc in next sc, 2 sc in next sc] 4 times—12 sc.

Round 12: Sc in each sc around.

Round 13: [Sc in next 2 sc, 2 sc in next sc] 4 times—16 sc.

Round 14: [Sc in next 3 sc, 2 sc in next sc] 4 times—20 sc.

Rounds 15 and 16: Sc in each sc around.

Round 17: [Sc in next 4 sc, 2 sc in next sc] 4 times—24 sc.

Rounds 18–27: Sc in each sc around.

Place two jingle bells inside Easter egg. Insert egg into body.

Round 28: [Sc in next 2 sc, sc2tog] 6 times—18 sc.

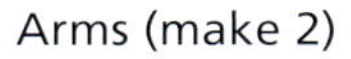

Round 29: [Sc2tog] 9 times—9 sc. Fasten off, leaving a long tail. With yarn needle, weave tail through stitches of last round. Pull gently, but firmly, to close opening. Tie securely, and weave in end.

Muzzle

Beginning at center front of muzzle, with smaller hook, ch 2.

Round 1 (RS): Work 4 sc in 2nd ch from hook; do *not* join and do *not* turn—4 sc. Place a marker to indicate the end of the round and move the marker up as each round is completed.

Round 2: Work 2 sc in each sc around—8 sc.

Rounds 3 and 4: Sc in each sc around. Fasten off, leaving a long tail for sewing.

Stuff muzzle and sew to lower front of head.

Ears (make 2)

With smaller hook, ch 5.

Row 1: Hdc in 2nd ch from hook, hdc in next ch, sc in next ch, 3 sc in last ch; rotate piece to work across opposite side of foundation ch (do *not* turn piece over, keep same side facing you), sc in next ch, hdc in last 2 ch—9 sts. Fasten off, leaving a long tail for sewing. Sew one ear to each side of head, toward the back.

Arms (make 2)

Beginning at top of arm, with smaller hook, ch 2.

Round 1: Work 6 sc in 2nd ch from hook; do *not* join and do *not* turn—6 sc. Place a marker to indicate the end of the round and move the marker up as each round is completed.

Rounds 2–4: Sc in each sc around.

Round 5: [Sc in next 2 sc, 2 sc in next sc] 2 times—8 sc.

Rounds 6–8: Sc in each sc around.

Stuff piece lightly.

Round 9: [Sc2tog] 4 times—4 sc. Fasten off, leaving a long tail. With yarn needle and long tail, sew one arm to each side of body, below neck.

Legs (make 2)

Beginning at top of leg, with smaller hook, ch 2.

Round 1 (RS): Work 8 sc in 2nd ch from hook; do *not* join and do *not* turn—8 sc. Place a marker to indicate the end of the round and move the marker up as each round is completed.

Round 2: Work 2 sc in each sc around—16 sc.

Round 3: [Sc in next 3 sc, 2 sc in next sc] 4 times—20 sc.
Stuff piece lightly. Continue to stuff piece as work progresses.
Rounds 4–6: Sc in each sc around.
Round 7: [Sc in next sc, sc2tog] 6 times, sc in next 2 sc—14 sc.
Round 8: [Sc in next sc, sc2tog] 4 times, sc in next 2 sc—10 sc.
Round 9: [Sc in next 3 sc, sc2tog] 2 times—8 sc.
Rounds 10 and 11: Sc in each sc around.
Round 12: [Sc in next 2 sc, 2 sc in next sc] 2 times, sc in next 2 sc—10 sc.
Rounds 13 and 14: Sc in each sc around.
Round 15: [Sc2tog] 5 times—5 sc.
Round 16: [Sc2tog] 2 times, sc in next sc—3 sc. Fasten off, leaving a very long tail.
With yarn needle, weave tail through stitches of last round. Pull gently, but firmly, to close opening. Tie securely, do *not* cut tail, use tail to shape and sew one leg to each side of body, as follows: Flatten top of leg (widest end) slightly and pin it to side of body, below arm. Fold leg slightly so the foot is positioned to floor and tack foot to leg. Sew leg to body. With yarn needle and another length of yarn, sew 2 lines into each foot to form toes. Weave in ends.

TAIL

Beginning at tip of tail, with smaller hook, ch 2.
Round 1: Work 5 sc in 2nd ch from hook—5 sc. Place a marker to indicate the end of the round and move the marker up as each round is completed.
Rounds 2–8: Sc in each sc around.
Round 9: Sc in next 2 sc, 2 sc in next sc, sc in next 2 sc—6 sc.
Rounds 10–12: Sc in each sc around. Fasten off, leaving a long tail for sewing. Stuff piece. With yarn needle, sew tail to bottom back, centered between legs. Weave in end.

FINISHING

With yarn needle and brown yarn, using photograph as a guide, embroider straight st eyes on face, above muzzle. Embroider straight st mouth at end of muzzle. Embroider straight st nostrils on muzzle, above mouth. Weave in any remaining ends. Place Joey inside Mama's pouch.•

ADORABLE POMPOM HAT

Easy

SIZES

6–12 (18–24) months.

MATERIALS

Yarn

Bernat® Softee® Baby Chunky™, 5oz/140g skeins, each approx 155yd/142m (acrylic)

- 1 (2) skeins in #96017 Nighty Night OR #96013 Creamsicle

Hook

- Size J/10 (6mm) crochet hook, *or size needed to obtain gauge*

GAUGE

12 sc and 13 rows = 4"/10cm using size J/10 (6mm) hook.

TAKE TIME TO CHECK GAUGE.

HAT

Ch 30 (32).

1st row: 1 sc in 2nd ch from hook. 1 sc in each ch to last 4 ch. Sl st in each of last 4 ch. Turn.

2nd row: Ch 1. Sl st in each of first 4 sts. 1 scbl in each st to end of row. Turn.

3rd row: Ch 1. 1 scbl in each st to last 4 sts. Sl st in each of last 4 sts. Turn.

Rep 2nd and 3rd rows until work measures 16 (17)"/40.5 (43)cm. Fasten off, leaving a long end. Weave end through last sl st of each row along top edge and gather tightly.

FINISHING

Sew back seam.

Pompoms (make 2)

Wind yarn around 4 fingers approx 100 times. Remove from fingers and tie tightly in center. Cut through each side of loops. Trim to smooth round shape. Attach pompom to each side of Hat as shown in photo.•

LIL BANDIT BLANKET

Easy

MEASUREMENTS

Approx 50 x 30"/127 x 76cm, excluding hood

MATERIALS

Yarn

Bernat® Softee® Baby Chunky™, 5oz/140g skeins, each approx 155yd/142m (acrylic)

- 6 skeins in #96005 Cozy Gray (MC)
- 2 skeins in #96017 Nighty Night (A)
- 1 skein in #96006 Cream Puff (B)

Hooks

- Sizes H/8 (5mm) and L/11 (8mm) crochet hooks, *or size needed to obtain gauge*

GAUGE

10 sts and 12 rows = 4"/10cm in pat using larger hook.
TAKE TIME TO CHECK GAUGE

NOTE

To join new color, work to last loops on hook of first color. Yoh with new color, draw through loops and proceed with new color.

BLANKET

With larger hook and B, ch 126.

1st row (RS): 1 sc in 2nd ch from hook. *Ch 1. Skip next ch. 1 sc in next ch. Rep from * to end of ch. Turn. 125 sts.

2nd row: Ch 1. 1 sc in first sc. 1 sc in next ch-1 sp. *Ch 1. Skip next sc. 1 sc in next ch-1 sp. Rep from * to last sc. 1 sc in last sc. Break B. Join A. Turn.

3rd row: With A, ch 1. 1 sc in first sc. *Ch 1. Skip next sc. 1 sc in next ch-1 sp. Rep from * to last 2 sc. Ch 1. Skip next sc. 1 sc in last sc. Turn.

4th row: With A, as 2nd row.

Last 2 rows form pat.

With A, work 4 more rows in pat.

With MC, cont in pat until work from beg measures approx 30"/76cm, ending on a WS row. Fasten off.

Hood

1st row (RS): With larger hook, join MC with sl st to 49th st of last row of Blanket. Ch 1. 1 sc in same sp as last sl st. 1 sc in each of next 26 sts. Turn. 27 sts.

2nd row: Ch 1. 1 sc in each sc to end of row. Turn.

3rd row: Ch 1. 1 sc in each of next 8 sc. 2 sc in each of next 2 sc. 1 sc in each of next 7 sc. 2 sc in each of next 2 sc. 1 sc in each of next 8 sc. Turn. 31 sc.

4th to 8th rows: Ch 1. 1 sc in each sc to end of row. Turn.

9th row: Ch 1. (1 sc in each of next 9 sc. 2 sc in each of next 2 sc) twice. 1 sc in each of next 9 sc. Turn. 35 sc.

10th to 14th rows: Ch 1. 1 sc in each sc to end of row. Turn.

15th row: Ch 1. 1 sc in each of next 10 sc. 2 sc in each of next 2 sc. 1 sc in each of next 11 sc. 2 sc in each of next 2 sc. 1 sc in each of next 10 sc. Turn. 39 sc.

Cont even in sc until Hood measures 8"/20.5cm, ending on a WS row. Fasten off.

LIL BANDIT BLANKET

Top of Hood

1st row (RS): With larger hook, join MC with sl st to 13th st of last row of Hood. Ch 1. 1 sc in same sp as last sl st. 1 sc in each of next 12 sc. Turn. 13 sc.

2nd and 3rd rows: Ch 1. 1 sc in each sc to end of row. Turn.

4th row: Ch 1. Sc2tog. 1 sc in each sc to last 2 sc. Sc2tog. 11 sc. Turn.

5th to 7th rows: Ch 1. 1 sc in each sc to end of row. Turn.

8th row: Ch 1. Sc2tog. 1 sc in each sc to last 2 sc. Sc2tog. 9 sc. Turn.

9th and 10th rows: Ch 1. 1 sc in each sc to end of row. Break MC at end of last row. Join A. Turn.

11th to 14th rows: With A, ch 1. 1 sc in each sc to end of row. Turn. Fasten off at end of 14th row. Sew sides of Top Hood to rem sts at either side of last row of Hood.

FINISHING

Border

With RS facing and larger hook, join B with sl st to any corner of Blanket.

1st rnd: Ch 1. Work sc evenly around entire edge of Blanket and front opening of Hood, having 3 sc in each corner. Join with sl st to first sc.

2nd rnd: Ch 1. Work 1 sc in each sc around, having 3 sc in each corner. Join with sl st to first sc. Fasten off.

Eyes (make 2)

With smaller hook and A, ch 2.

1st rnd: 6 sc in 2nd ch from hook. Join with sl st to first sc. Fasten off. With B, embroider French Knot (see page 10) in center of Eye.

Nose

With smaller hook and B, ch 2.

1st rnd: 6 sc in 2nd ch from hook. Join with sl st to first sc. Fasten off.

Ears

Inner ears (make 2)

With smaller hook and A, ch 2.

1st row (RS): 5 sc in 2nd ch from hook. Turn.

2nd row: Ch 1. 2 sc in each sc across. 10 sc. Turn.

3rd row: Ch 1. 1 sc in each of first 4 sc. (1 hdc. 1 dc) in next sc. (1 dc. 1 hdc) in next sc. 1 sc in each of next 4 sc. Fasten off.

Outer ears (make 2)

With MC and smaller hook, make as given for Inner Ear.

With WS of Inner Ear and Outer ear facing each other, and RS of Inner Ear facing, join B with sl st to first sc.

1st row: Ch 1. Working through both thicknesses, 1 sc in each of first 4 sc. 2 hdc in next st. (2 dc. 1 tr) in next st. (1 tr. 2 dc) in next st. 2 hdc in next st. 1 sc in each of next 4 sts. Fasten off.

FINISHING

Sew Eyes, Nose and Ears to Hood as seen in picture.•

DUCK TOY

Easy

MEASUREMENTS

Approx 4"/10cm square

MATERIALS

Yarn (4)

Bernat® Handicrafter Cotton®, 1¾oz/50g skeins, each approx 84yd/77m (cotton)

- 2 skeins in #01030 Pale Yellow

Hook

- Size G/6 (4mm) crochet hook, *or size needed to obtain gauge*

Notions

- Ribbon 14"/35.5cm long, 3/8"/1cm wide
- Stuffing
- Blue embroidery thread

GAUGE

18 sc and 20 rows = 4"/10cm using size G/6 (4mm) hook.
TAKE TIME TO CHECK GAUGE.

DUCK TOY

Front/Back (make 2 pieces alike)

Ch 11.

1st row (RS): 1 sc in 2nd ch from hook. 1 sc in each ch to end of ch. Turn. 10 sc.

2nd row: Ch 1. 2 sc in first sc. 1 sc in each sc to last sc. 2 sc in last sc. Turn.

Rep last row 3 times more, ending with 18 sc.

Next row: Ch 1. 1 sc in each sc to end of row. Turn.

Rep last row 6 times more.

Tail

Next row (RS): Ch 1. 1 sc in each of next 6 sc. Sc2tog. Turn. Leave rem sts unworked.

Next row: Ch 1. Sc2tog. 1 sc in each of next 3 sc. Sc2tog. Turn.

Next row: Ch 1. Sc2tog. 1 sc in next sc. Sc2tog. Turn.

Next row: Ch 1. 1 sc in first sc. Sc2tog. Turn.

Next row: Ch 1. Sc2tog. Fasten off.

Head

With WS of work facing, join yarn with sl st to first st. Ch 1. 1 sc in same sp as sl st. 1 sc in each of next 8 sc. Sc2tog. Turn.

Next row: Ch 1. Sc2tog. 1 sc in each of next 8 sc. Turn.

Next row: Ch 1. Sc2tog. 1 sc in each of next 5 sc. Sc2tog. Turn. 7 sc.

Next row: Ch 1. 3 sc in first st. 1 sc in each sc to last 2 sts. Sc2tog. Turn. 8 sc.

Next row: Ch 1. 2 sc in first st. 1 sc in each sc to last st. 2 sc. Turn. 10 sc.

Next row: Ch 1. 1 sc in each sc to end of row. Ch 2. Turn.

Next row: 1 sc in 2nd ch from hook. 1 sc in each sc to end of row. Turn.

Rep last 2 rows twice more. 13 sc.

Next row: Ch 1. Sc2tog. 1 sc in each of next 5 sc. Sc2tog. Turn.

Next row: Ch 1. Sc2tog. 1 sc in each of next 3 sc. Sc2tog. Turn.

Next row: Ch 1. Sc2tog. Sc3tog. Fasten off.

FINISHING

Joining Back and Front

Place Back and Front tog. Join yarn with sl st to first ch of foundation ch, working through both thicknesses. Ch 1. 1 sc in same sp as sl st. 1 sc in each sp around, stuffing lightly as you work 3 sc in top of Tail and point of nose. Join with sl st to first sc. Fasten off.

With blue thread, embroider eye as shown in picture.
Tie ribbon around neck.•

NEW YEAR TIGER

Easy

MEASUREMENTS

Approx 7"/18cm tall

MATERIALS

Yarn (4)

Lily® Sugar'n Cream, 2½oz/71g skeins, each approx 120yd/109m (cotton)

- 1 skein each in #01004 Soft Ecru (A), #01130 Warm Brown (B), and #01628 Hot Orange (C)

Hook

- Size E/4 (3.5mm) crochet hook, *or size needed to obtain gauge*

Notions

- Stuffing
- 2 small black beads for eyes
- Small amount of black embroidery floss

GAUGE

16 sc and 20 rows = 4"/10cm using size E/4 (3.5mm) hook.

TAKE TIME TO CHECK GAUGE.

STRIPE PATTERN

With B, work 1 rnd. With C, work 2 rnds.

These 3 rnds form Stripe Pat.

TIGER

Head

**With A, ch 2.

1st rnd: 6 sc in 2nd ch from hook. Join with sl st to first sc.

2nd rnd: Ch 1. 2 sc in each sc around. Join with sl st to first sc. 12 sc.

3rd rnd: Ch 1. *2 sc in next sc. 1 sc in next sc. Rep from * around. Join with sl st to first sc. 18 sc.

4th rnd: Ch 1. 1 sc in each sc around. Join B with sl st to first sc.

5th rnd: With B, ch 1. 2 sc in each sc around. Join C with sl st to first sc. 36 sc.

6th rnd: With C, ch 1. 1 sc in each sc around. Join with sl st to first sc.

First 2 rnds of Stripe Pat are complete. Keeping cont of Stripe Pat, rep last rnd 7 times more.

Keeping cont of Stripe Pat, proceed as follows:

Next rnd: Ch 1. *Draw up a loop in each of next 2 sc. Yoh and draw through all loops on hook—sc2tog made. 1 sc in each of next 4 sc. Rep from * around. Join with sl st to first sc. 30 sts.

Next rnd: Ch 1. 1 sc in each sc around. Join with sl st to first sc.

Next rnd: Ch 1. *Sc2tog. 1 sc in next sc. Rep from * around. Join with sl st to first sc. 20 sts.

Stuff Head.

Next rnd: Ch 1. *Sc2tog. Rep from * around. Join with sl st to first st. Fasten off. 10 sts.

Stuff rem of Head. Draw yarn through rem sts. Pull tightly and fasten securely.

First Leg

With A, ch 2.

1st rnd: 6 sc in 2nd ch from hook. Join with sl st to first sc.

2nd rnd: Ch 1. 2 sc in each sc around. Join with sl st to first sc. 12 sc.

3rd rnd: Ch 1. 1 sc in each sc around. Join B with sl st to first sc.

4th rnd: With B, as 3rd rnd.

First rnd of Stripe Pat is complete.

Keeping cont of Stripe Pat, rep last rnd 3 times more.

Fasten off at end of last rnd.

Second Leg

Work as for First Leg. Do *not* fasten off.

Keeping cont of Stripe Pat, cont as follows for Body:

Body

Next rnd: Ch 1. 1 sc in each of next 6 sc of Second Leg. Sl st in first sc of First Leg. 1 sc in same sp as sl st. 1 sc in each of next 11 sc of First Leg. 1 sc in each of last 6 sc of Second Leg. Join with sl st to first sc. 24 sc.

Next rnd: Ch 1. 1 sc in each st around. Join with sl st to first sc. Keeping cont of Stripe Pat, rep last rnd 5 times more.

NEW YEAR TIGER

Next rnd: Ch 1. *Sc2tog. 1 sc in each of next 4 sc. Rep from * around. Join with sl st to first sc. 20 sts.

Next rnd: Ch 1. 1 sc in each sc around. Join with sl st to first sc.

Rep last rnd once more.

Next rnd: Ch 1. *Sc2tog. 1 sc in each of next 3 sc. Rep from * around. Join with sl st to first sc. 16 sts.

Next rnd: Ch 1. *Sc2tog. 1 sc in each of next 2 sts. Rep from * around. Join with sl st to first sc. 12 sts. Fasten off.

Stuff Body and Legs.

Tummy

With A, ch 2.

1st rnd: 8 sc in 2nd ch from hook. Join with sl st to first sc.

2nd rnd: Ch 1. 2 sc in each sc around. Join with sl st to first sc. 16 sc.

3rd rnd: Ch 1. 1 sc in each sc around. Join with sl st to first sc.

Fasten off.

With black embroidery floss, embroider belly button.

Stuff Tummy lightly and sew to front of Body as shown in picture.

Arms (make 2)

With A, ch 2.

****1st rnd:** 6 sc in 2nd ch from hook. Join with sl st to first sc.

2nd rnd: Ch 1. *2 sc in next sc. 1 sc in next sc. Rep from * around. Join with sl st to first sc. 9 sc.

3rd rnd: Ch 1. 1 sc in each sc around. Join B with sl st to first sc.

4th rnd: With B, as 3rd rnd.** First rnd of Stripe Pat is complete. Keeping cont of Stripe Pat, rep last rnd 5 times more. Fasten off.

Stuff Arms lightly.

Ears (make 2)

With C, ch 2. Work as given from ** to ** for Arms, omitting references to color changes. Fasten off at end of last rnd.

Tail

Work as given for Arms. Stuff Tail lightly.

FINISHING

Sew Head to Body. Attach Ears to top of Head. Attach Arms to sides of Body. Attach Tail to back of Body. Sew beads to front of Head for Eyes. With black embroidery floss, embroider nose and mouth.•